04/07

I0373329

203.
Naylor, Sharon.
Renewing your wedding vows
a complete planning guide t
saying, "I still do"
New York : Broadway Books,
2006.

RENEWING YOUR WEDDING VOWS

Discarded by
Santa Maria Library

SANTA MARIA PUBLIC LIBRARY

5/07

ADDITIONAL BOOKS BY SHARON NAYLOR

The Bridesmaid Handbook

1000 Best Wedding Bargains

1000 Best Secrets for Your Perfect Wedding

Your Special Wedding Toasts

Your Special Wedding Vows

The Mother-of-the-Bride Book

Mother of the Groom

The Groom's Guide

Your Day, Your Way: The Essential Handbook for the 21st Century Bride (coauthor)

The Ultimate Bridal Shower Idea Book

The New Honeymoon Planner

How to Have a Fabulous Wedding for $10,000 or Less

The Complete Outdoor Wedding Planner

How to Plan an Elegant Wedding in 6 Months or Less

1001 Ways to Have a Dazzling Second Wedding

The 52 Most Romantic Places In and Around New York City (contributor)

It's My Wedding Too: A Novel

and others as listed at www.sharonnaylor.net

Renewing YOUR WEDDING VOWS

A COMPLETE PLANNING GUIDE TO SAYING
"I Still Do"

SHARON NAYLOR

BROADWAY BOOKS

NEW YORK

RENEWING YOUR WEDDING VOWS. Copyright © 2006 by Sharon Naylor.
All rights reserved. No part of this book may be reproduced or transmitted in any form
or by any means, electronic or mechanical, including photocopying, recording, or
by any information storage and retrieval system, without written permission from the
publisher. For information, address Broadway Books, a division of Random House, Inc.

PRINTED IN THE UNITED STATES OF AMERICA

BROADWAY BOOKS and its logo, a letter B bisected on the
diagonal, are trademarks of Random House, Inc.

Visit our Web site at www.broadwaybooks.com

LIBRARY OF CONGRESS CATALOGING-IN-PUBLICATION DATA
Naylor, Sharon.
Renewing your wedding vows : a complete planning guide to saying "I *still* do" /
Sharon Naylor.—1st ed.
p.   cm.
Includes index.
1. Marriage service. I. Title.

BL619.M37N395 2006
203'.85—dc22
2006040169

ISBN-13: 978-0-7679-2321-7
ISBN-10: 0-7679-2321-9

1 3 5 7 9 10 8 6 4 2

FIRST EDITION

CREDITS

Photos: pages 19, 85, 103, 161, 167, 171, and 187 courtesy of Casey Cooper, Botanicals Inc,
www.botanicalschicago.com; page 149 courtesy of Ron Ben-Israel Wedding Cakes,
www.weddingcakes.com; page 174 courtesy of Dana Smith-Acosta,
www.charmingfavours.com; page 10 wedding photo courtesy of Alain Brin, renewal photo
courtesy of Sonya Melescu at www.virginislandsphoto.com; page 20 courtesy of Douglas
Kaufman; page 26 courtesy of Phil Kissinger, Photos by Phil; page 44 courtesy of Suzanne
Venino; page 54 wedding photo courtesy of Raul Gonzales, renewal photo courtesy of
Isabel Ibarra; page 80 courtesy of Andrew and Joanne Blahitka; page 86 courtesy of Sonya
Melesen; page 94 courtesy of Carol and Jeff Cohen; page 104 courtesy of Michael
Molinoff; page 112 courtesy of Paul Toepfer Photography in Verona, WI; page 120 wedding
photo courtesy of Robert Kerr, renewal photo courtesy of Windstar Cruises; page 128
courtesy of Paul Toepfer Photography in Verona, WI; page 134 courtesy of Terry and
T. J. Jankowski; page 150 courtesy of Heidi Olson; page 162 courtesy of David Kramer,
Kramer Photography, NJ; page 172 courtesy of Tina Tessina and Richard Sharrard;
page 180 courtesy of Sacco Productions; page 188 courtesy of Jennifer and Greg Grizzle;
page 204 courtesy of Susanne Alexander and Craig Farnsworth. Invitation: page 192
courtesy of Jennifer and Greg Grizzle, created by Paper Affair in Atlanta

THIS BOOK IS DEDICATED TO:

Millie & Bill

Augie & Mary

Annie & Nick

Sue & Vic

Terry & George

Jill & Mark

Pam & Ron

Jen & Troy

and

Joanne & Andy

CONTENTS

ACKNOWLEDGMENTS

With many thanks, hugs, and toasts to the following wonderful people who have made this book possible . . .

- My visionary editor, Trish Medved at Broadway Books, as well as her fabulous assistants, Beth Adams and Lea Beresford
- My loyal and trustworthy agent, Meredith Bernstein
- Publicity genius, Scott Buhrmaster, who knows how to make things happen
- My always-dependable Webmaster, Mike Napolitan
- My colleagues and friends at the American Society of Journalists and Authors, the Association of Bridal Consultants, and the International Special Events Society
- Erik and Beth Kent of NJWedding.com
- And the many wedding experts and real-life married couples who generously devoted their time and shared their stories for this book

If all you say is Thank You, that's enough . . .

INTRODUCTION

"I'd marry you all over again."

Do you know how many single women (and men) out there dream of having the loving marriage with a wonderful spouse who would say *that* to them? "You're so lucky!" they'd sigh with just a touch of green-eyed envy. But you and I know that it's not luck that's behind your still-going-strong marriage. It's effort. It's investing time, and matching deed to word. It's not just remembering your wedding vows, but living them every day. You're together because you kept your word. Everything you promised on your wedding day—to love each other in good times and in bad, in sickness and in health, for richer and for poorer—you've both delivered on.

If that's not something to celebrate, I don't know what is!

Sure, you celebrate your wedding anniversary every year. You may go to dinner, exchange gifts, have breakfast in bed, clink champagne glasses, or maybe even eat Chinese takeout food on the couch while watching a great movie (perhaps your wedding video). But this year . . . *this year* . . . that heartfelt whisper of "I'd marry you all over again" could become a reality.

You can renew your wedding vows.

Imagine gathering all of your friends and family (and your children) together to witness and celebrate your wedding vow renewal ceremony. Imagine walking down the aisle again in a beautiful gown, carrying a breathtaking bouquet, and once again seeing that amazed and grateful look in your husband's eyes the first time he sees you that day. It's even more meaningful now.

Imagine standing before him and speaking aloud your appreciation for him and for what you have now that you had only *hoped* would be part of the "happily ever after" you dreamed of on your wedding day.

Now imagine the words *he* will say to you, all of those wonderful terms of endearment, his heartfelt promises to you and what he now dreams of for your long and happy future together. Don't you just love the sound of his voice? Don't you love hearing him tell you what you mean to him? Imagine the kiss as you re-seal your wedding vows to the sounds of applause from everyone who loves you.

George Sand's immortal words "The only happiness in life is to love and be loved" are so true. Love is the only true happiness in life, and you have it. In abundance. At your wedding vow renewal ceremony, *everyone* gets a reminder of just how wonderful it is to be loved, to express love, and to be lucky enough to see it in action. That's why renewing wedding vows is such a growing trend today. We want to celebrate what's *good* in our lives. We want to honor our spouses, our marriages, the lives we've built together, our happily ever after. We want the spotlight on true love stories, not the fleeting newsflashes and bitter gossip of celebrity marriage and divorces.

Across the country and the world, married couples are planning their own wedding vow renewal ceremonies and receptions. Whether they've been married for one year, five years, ten years, fifty years (or more!), they're planning what can truly be called the celebration of a lifetime. Celebrating a lifetime shared or a lifetime still unfolding, all with the added bliss of having your family and friends share in the moment . . . that's the icing on the three-tiered chocolate mousse–filled cake.

> "A marriage vow renewal ceremony is a way to begin your marriage anew. Many couples express that their wedding renewal was more deeply meaningful than their original wedding service because there is so much more life experience since the day they first married. Whether you've been married one year or fifty, it's important to express your appreciation for each other and give the gift of a new beginning."
>
> —*Anne Marie Porter, a wedding officiant on St. John's in the U.S. Virgin Islands*

Why Have a Vow Renewal Ceremony?

You loved it so much the first time, you want to do it again.

Or, something went wrong the first time (such as a big rainstorm that moved your outdoor wedding inside), and you want that sunset ceremony on the beach.

Some couples tell me that this is their chance to have the wedding they always wanted, the one they were too young to request when they first married and their parents were in charge. This is their do-over. They'll finally get to have their big day.

While some couples see their fifteenth or twentieth anniversary approaching and think, "Wouldn't it be *fantastic* to renew our vows," other couples discover the possibilities after the storm clouds have passed in their lives . . . after a trauma or tragedy that makes them take stock of all that's most precious to them. For instance, think about the husband who supports his wife through her breast cancer diagnosis and chemotherapy treatments. The one person he loves most in the world almost left him, and now that she's recovering and perhaps in remission, he wants to marry her all over again.

Think about the military couple who haven't seen each other in a year, with one of them deployed into a frightening danger zone and the other holding down the fort in superhuman fashion while waiting patiently for his or her safe return. When the plane arrives or the ship sails in, and the loved one has returned, there's no one on earth who matters more. They'd marry each other all over again.

Then there is the couple who fought the good fight, who worked their way through a time of estrangement and difficulty in their marriage to heal their wounds. Many other people would have given up and gotten divorced, but this couple did the hard work and soul-searching, the apologizing and the valiant earning back of trust and respect. They too have much to celebrate, and the renewing of their vows is an important symbolic step in their relationship.

AFTER THE STORM CLEARS . . .

"You might wish to renew your vows to celebrate a special anniversary or you may feel it's appropriate to renew your vows after a challenging time that tested your relationship, such as a period of separation, a serious illness, problems with a child, or a job loss. Or it may be a tragedy you've overcome, such as a fire or hurricane that destroyed your home and everything in it. You may have lost everything, but you still have each other. These are natural times to reaffirm your commitment to one another.

—*Rosanna McCollough, editor-in-chief of WeddingChannel.com*

Do you see yourselves in these situations? Have you had a tough year as well, only to grow more in love with and more dedicated to your spouse? Life can be a rough roller-coaster ride for so many of us, and it's a triumph when we beat the odds. It's a shared triumph when you do it hand-in-hand with your spouse. One way to mark your shared triumph is to renew your vows.

I've written this book to help you plan your own celebration. I'm thrilled for you that whatever your story and whatever challenges you've overcome, you're living your happily ever after. It's my *honor* to help you plan your renewal ceremony and the party afterward. You'll find out where to start, how to choose the perfect style of celebration for you, what the etiquette is for today's vow renewal ceremonies, what to wear, and all of the fun things like choosing a cake and picking out flowers. You'll get the same thrill out of finding the perfect gown or checking out caterers, designing centerpieces and shopping for the perfect favors as today's first-time brides.

"There's an excitement about planning a wedding vow renewal ceremony and celebration that can be even greater than when you planned the wedding. After all, you know yourself better, you know your spouse better, the relationship is established, and there's a higher level of intimacy in hearing the words now. It can be more meaningful the second time around. Plus, with perhaps more disposable income now and no one influencing you, you're free to have the celebration you always wanted, whether it's a large or intimate event. You might want to travel and enjoy the kinds of romantic and exciting vow renewal packages the resort industry offers—cruises, getaways to tropical islands or overseas destinations, wherever you desire. You're not limited to your living room, so you can state your commitment to one another anywhere on earth you can imagine."

—*Rosanna McCollough, editor-in-chief of WeddingChannel.com*

Could it get better than this? Yes, actually . . . There is another perk.

As your children or grandchildren look on at your vow renewal ceremony, they get to see what a real commitment looks like. They get proof that with hard work, love, and understanding, there *is* such a thing as a marriage that lasts. We live in such a disposable society, after all, where marriages are "won" on television shows and where some celebrities' hairstyles last longer than their marriages. Actually, some celebrities' *lunches* last longer than their marriages. The younger generation unfortunately sees all too often that marriage is out of fashion, that "it just doesn't work" in today's world. They see it in their friends' parents' marriages, in movies and TV shows, and on the pages of gossip magazines. They—and *we*—are bombarded every day with stories of unhappy splits and the rising divorce rate.

It's time to show them a relationship that's real, one that's worked, and at the same time be role models to them. For example, twenty-year-old Lila attended her parents' twenty-fifth wedding vow renewal ceremony and took more away from that splendid day than a simple silver frame favor. She says:

I just saw how happy they were as they stood up there holding hands and smiling so amazingly at each other. My father winked as he wiped a tear from my mother's cheek and he told her how much he appreciated her in his life, how he wanted to share the secret that he often stops in the doorway before he comes home and says a silent "thank you" for the woman he's coming home to. My mother told him that she's happy for the wrinkles she's gotten because he always makes her laugh so much.

And it hit me . . . I just thought, "I want that. I want to be adored like that." So I broke up with the guy I was seeing, the one who couldn't be bothered to come to my parents' vow renewal ceremony with me, and promised myself that I would only date a man who treats me with value and respect, and makes me smile. I raised my own standards that day and know that I'll find the love of my life sometime soon. I now know what I'm looking for.

If you're a parent, think about the benefits of this celebration for your kids, maybe even your grandkids. In addition, think about how you might, through your example, inspire the silently hurting *adults* you invite to your celebration, those who have been stung by the risk of loving and are—make that *were*—afraid to hope for a lasting marriage for themselves. You truly have no idea how deeply your example will touch others. And someday, you might find yourselves at *their* vow renewal ceremonies as well . . . maybe even being thanked or toasted for the glorious illustration of "happily ever after" you set for them way back when.

In fact, in today's world of wedding vow renewals, the *children* might plan the event as a gift to their parents. Perhaps they know a big anniversary is coming up for their parents, and they know that Mom and Dad are a bit modest. They'd never plan a party in their own honor. Their example means so much to their children. It has enhanced their own lives and given them a strong foundation for which they're grateful. They can think of no better way to honor their parents.

Another trend is for one spouse to surprise the other with a vow renewal celebration that he or she has planned. It's a surprise party with a twist. These days, it's the *husbands* who are looking into this option more than ever, wanting to give their wives a day to remember. The men spend months planning the celebration, choosing the cake and the menu, inviting guests, even going as far as buying the wives new dresses or new jewelry to wear for a "nice dinner out" (wink, wink). That romantic husband has just set the bar high for every other man in attendance. (See page 128 for the renewal celebration Dr. Chris Kammer planned for his wife, Jean Marie, on the occasion of their twentieth wedding anniversary.)

Another surprise trend: the renewal celebration awaits on a tropical island. You've flown in the kids, the grandkids, your friends, parents, and original bridal party. That summer vacation your spouse was expecting becomes so much more when the surprise is revealed.

In the past few years, new ways of celebrating vow renewals have emerged as more and more couples embrace the idea of celebrating what's *right* in their relationships. From big wedding do-overs to intimate, "just us" private celebrations on a hillside or at home, there are as many ways to create the ceremony as there are reasons for doing it.

Part 1

DEFINING YOUR STYLE

BRAD AND LYNDEE BUCHANAN, MARRIED FEBRUARY 2, 2000,
RENEWED NOVEMBER 19, 2002

"Our family started with our wedding on February 2, 2000, at Hawksnest Beach in St. John, U.S. Virgin Islands. From the moment we set foot on the ferry dock on Cruz Bay, I knew we had picked the perfect place to get married. Our wedding coordinator canceled on us at the last minute, and we were referred to an officiant who would marry us on Hawksnest Beach. We agreed, sight unseen. We made all the arrangements via telephone and Internet. The day could not have been more perfect. We wanted a spiritual and intimate ceremony, and we only included elements that were special to us. After our ceremony, our coordinator, Anne Marie, mentioned how great it would be if we returned to Hawksnest Beach sometime in the future to christen our first child. We left our hearts there and dreamed about the day we would bring our child to our own personal paradise.

"On November 19, 2002, we took Anne Marie up on her suggestion and brought our daughter, Lauryn, to Hawksnest Beach, where we had her christened in the exact same place where we started our life together. It felt so beautiful to christen her at our special place and to have her join us as we renewed our wedding vows standing in the azure blue St. John's waters with Anne Marie leading us once again. Even better, Lauryn wore the same baptism dress that I wore as a baby . . . which, incidentally, happened on February 2, 1972, our wedding anniversary!

"Our son, Brandon Tyler, was born on October 17, 2004, and he was also christened on Hawksnest Beach. We've just celebrated our fifth wedding anniversary, and we'll return to the paradise of St. John's to renew our vows as a family of four."

1

WHAT KIND OF VOW RENEWAL
CELEBRATION DO YOU WANT?

Imagine standing in front of a waterfall . . . in Hawaii. You have a hibiscus flower tucked behind your ear; your shoulders are tan and you're in a white sundress with a pink and white flower lei around your neck. Your husband takes your hand and tells you he'll love you forever as a dozen of your closest friends and family look on with tears in their eyes. Behind them, a rainbow arches over the clear sky, diving into the azure blue ocean.

Or . . .

Imagine once again walking down the aisle in the same church or synagogue where you were originally married. You're carrying a bouquet of white gardenias and roses just like those you had at your wedding. Your friends and family—all two hundred of them—stand as you walk by, escorted by your sons. Your husband smiles at you with pure adoration in his eyes, overwhelmed by how beautiful you are as you approach. You both repeat the very same vows you spoke twenty years ago, and they mean even more to you now.

So what do you have in mind as your wedding vow renewal celebration style? Something small and simple? A getaway to a tropical island? A do-over of your wedding day, but even better? What's so wonderful about this celebration is that it's yours to dream up and design any way you wish.

You've undoubtedly heard about various celebrities' wedding vow renewals—like Celine Dion's $1.5 million *Arabian Nights*–themed extravaganza in Las Vegas for her fourth anniversary with husband, René Angelil (where costumed servants carried Ms. Dion into the room like a queen), or Madonna and Guy Ritchie's reported do-over "after a rough year." These extravagant bashes definitely have an inspiring role in the growing trend of wedding vow renewal ceremonies today. But not all couples are copying celebrity style for their own celebrations. The choice of vow renewal ceremony and reception style is unlimited in possibilities and completely individual and personal. Just look at the following examples of real-life vow renewal celebrations, at the wildly varying range of style and formalities and themes. In a moment, you'll start creating your own picture for your own . . .

The Wedding You Never Had—Back when you were newly engaged, you imagined an elegant wedding in a hotel's ballroom, with ice sculptures, a harpist playing at the cocktail hour, a seafood buffet, a designer gown, a five-tiered cake . . . but it wasn't meant to be. Back then, your parents were in charge of the wedding (they were paying for it), so the event was more *them* than *you*. It's always something that's been in your mind, that you wished you would have spoken up and requested more of your own choices. But you stayed quiet then. It was a lovely wedding, even if it didn't include some of the things you dreamed of. And you still married the man of your dreams, so who's complaining? Now, though, your wedding vow renewal ceremony is going to be everything you wanted back then and more. The harpist you didn't have then will be playing at your cocktail hour now. Your gown will be more sophisticated, not the puffball you look at in horror in your wedding pictures. (It's not your fault . . . Vera Wang wasn't around then.) This celebration will be your dream come true. You have the resources now to make it happen for yourselves, and it's going to be wonderful to celebrate the way you've always wanted. So bring on the limousines, the fine wines and champagnes, the sushi station, and the sage green invitations with dark green engraved print. You get a second chance.

Something Out in Nature—Forget the ballroom and the expensive champagne. What's really *you* would be gathering everyone together at a scenic overview with a beautiful view of the ocean, the desert, or the mountains, or by a lake.

On the Beach—There's a reason so many weddings take place at oceanside, and it's the same reason so many wedding vow renewal ceremonies are also planned as beach celebrations. You'll take your vows barefoot in the sand as everyone looks on, as the ocean waves curl and rush to shore, and then after you seal your vows with a kiss, you'll join hands and walk along the beach together.

The Destination Renewal—This style is quickly becoming a favorite of first-time brides and grooms who fly a handful of their closest guests to a tropical island. Your renewal celebration could be the same exact style . . . with all of the island resort perks like steel drum players setting the tone for your walk toward the officiant.

THE WORLD IS WAITING . . .

Island resorts are opening their doors to you with vow renewal or second honeymoon packages that may be better than your original honeymoon. Massages on the beach may be included, and your getaway ride is a pair of white horses on the beach. All as part of the package. In addition to the dream island getaway, another option is going out to the American West, standing before majestic desert rock formations in Arizona, or out in Big Sky Country of Montana before mountainous vistas and in wide-open spaces. Such a getaway makes your destination vow renewal event a great adventure for all of your guests.

A Cruise—Now you can book a wedding vow renewal cruise, a special package designed by many cruise lines to include a ceremony officiated by the ship's captain, either out on deck or in a formal dining room, even in the onboard chapel. You'll often receive a bottle of champagne to celebrate, take-home champagne flutes to commemorate your renewal, a bouquet and boutonniere, a two- or three-tiered wedding cake, live or recorded music to set the scene, and photography and videography. Some cruise lines offer onshore excursions in their ports of call, so you could renew your vows onboard and then celebrate with your guests in Cancun, Hawaii, Europe, Canada, the Bahamas, even Alaska for quite a grand and exciting backdrop to your celebration.

A City Loft—It's your *Renewal and the City* party, with chic décor, Asian fusion food, cosmopolitans or mojitos, a view of the city lights at night, and everyone's dressed fabulously. A sophisticated, trendy party at a friend's amazing loft (which could be your "something borrowed" this time around)—or at one of the many stylish lofts that you can rent for your party—might be just your style. You often go into the city to enjoy the culture and nightlife, the great restaurants and entertainment, so there's no other theme you'd rather enjoy for your own celebration than one that reflects your shared interests.

A Dessert and Champagne Party—You've laughed together after attending relatives' and friends' weddings that you would have been happy with just the desserts and the cake. You're both decadent in your tastes—you love chocolate and a fine champagne. So your evening party will be all about the cake, the tiramisu, and the chocolate-covered strawberries.

A Brunch—Sunday morning could bring you to a restaurant or hotel's ballroom for a lavish brunch with dozens of food stations, mimosas, omelets and crepes to order, and a killer dessert bar in addition to your wedding cake. This morning celebration could be held right after church where your vows would be renewed by the same officiant who originally married you.

A Backyard Gathering—You don't need to dress up and drink champagne. You're happiest in jeans and a T-shirt, and so are your family and friends. So you could plan an informal backyard gathering, fire up the barbecue grill, cook up some ribs and chicken and mahi mahi, portabello mushrooms and shrimp kebabs, and set the blender to its daiquiri setting. A family-style barbecue gives you just the comfy at-home celebration you wanted, and the garden you planted, the trellis you tended, are the perfect backdrop for your day.

A Simple, Private Ceremony at Home—Your dream is to descend your staircase to the tune of "the wedding march," repeat your vows in front of the fireplace, then gather with the family around the dining room table. This style brings yet another in a long line of special family celebrations to your home.

By no means are these the only options. They're simply the ones most popular right now. We all want to celebrate our happiest moments in environments and in styles that are most *us*. And envisioning your ideal style and theme is the next step toward your own planning process.

Your Style Checklist

Start building your renewal celebration right here. Sit down together during some downtime, maybe grab a glass of wine or a cup of coffee, and consider your options *as a team* so that the event is wonderfully reflective of your partnership. Your kids can certainly help you along the way, turning this process into a terrific family activity. Your children may have special skills that you can use. One might be a musician and can advise on creating a personalized song list. One might have a knack for catering or for graphic arts. Bringing in the family to co-plan can add even deeper levels of meaning to the ceremony and reception.

The checklist on the following pages will start setting the foundation for your event, taking you step-by-step through the most fundamental decisions. Feel free to make extra notes in the margins and between sections—you're your own event planner, so you know what special ideas you have already!

The Size of Your Celebration

WE WANT:

- ☐ A very small party, only immediate family and closest friends
- ☐ A small party, under 30 people
- ☐ A medium-sized party, 30–50 people

- ☐ A large party, 50–75 people
- ☐ A larger party, 75–100 people
- ☐ A huge party, 100–150 people
- ☐ Everyone we've ever known

For the Ceremony

You'll find more on building your ceremony in Part 2. For now, we're just talking about style.

WE WANT:

- ☐ A religious ceremony, led by a religious officiant
- ☐ A spiritual ceremony, led by a spiritual officiant
- ☐ A secular ceremony, led by a nonreligious officiant
- ☐ A secular ceremony, led by a family member or friend
- ☐ We'll create and lead our own vow renewal ceremony

The Formality Level

We'll talk more about what you'll be wearing in Part 3, with complete wardrobe advice. For now, I'd like you to use the image of what you'd like to wear as a tool to define the formality of the event itself. After all, just as with weddings, the formality of the celebration will determine many factors such as the location and décor of your party, the style of the invitations you'll send, favors you'll give, the style of catering you'll choose, and so on. It's all connected, so think about the category of formality that's *most comfortable for you.*

WE WANT:

- ☐ Ultraformal (think of an ultraformal wedding, with the bride in long, floor-length gown and the men in tuxedoes wearing white gloves)
- ☐ Formal (think gowns for the women and tuxedoes or suits for the men)
- ☐ Semiformal (think gowns or cocktail-length dresses for the ladies and suits for the men)
- ☐ Informal (think street-length dresses for the women, suits or jackets for the men)

☐ Casual (sundresses for the women, and jeans, tee shirts, khaki pants and white shirts for the men; a very laid-back affair)

The Budget

We'll get into your budget in Chapter 4, but it's a guiding principle to state your expected expense level right now. Money may be a factor for your plans, or it might not. Either way, it's best for you both to discuss your clear expectations for what this event will cost so that the very marriage you're celebrating doesn't become strained over the very real pull of spending "just a little bit more to make it extra special." State your wishes now, and then vow to stay *close* to what you'd originally discussed:

WE WANT:

☐ A lower budget affair, no more than $_____. It's the meaning of the day that matters most.

☐ A moderate budget. This is a special event, after all . . .

☐ A sizable budget. Hey, we're worth it!

Sun Factor

WE WANT:

☐ Outdoor

☐ Indoor

Do You Know the Time?

WE WANT:

☐ A morning event

☐ An afternoon event

☐ An early-evening event

☐ An evening event

☐ A late-night event

What's Your Season?

We'll cover choosing the date for your vow renewal celebration in Chapter 3, but I'm including the question of season here to get you thinking. There's no rule that says you have to hold your celebration on your actual wedding anniversary, after all. If you had a summer wedding, you're not restricted to holding your renewal celebration in the summer.

WE WANT:

- ☐ Spring
- ☐ Summer
- ☐ Autumn
- ☐ Winter

ED AND MOLLY BUCKLEY, MARRIED JUNE 4, 1994.

RENEWED IN JULY OF 2004

"We took our vows underwater, with the same minister who married us ten years ago diving down to conduct our renewal ceremony. Speakers on our masks transmitted what we were saying to all of our guests above water, and we celebrated with friends and family in a great, casual atmosphere outdoors. We love being by the water, since we run a dive shop on St. Croix, so this was a terrific way to share our celebration with them."

2

SHARING THE MOMENT

Just as important as the moment you'll share with each other when you take your vows once again, are the people who will be standing there with you as witnesses to that moment. The vast majority of the couples I spoke to, whether they renewed their vows after one year or fifty, said that what made the day immensely more special to them was the presence of their children, their grandchildren, their parents, sisters, brothers, family, and friends. Many couples will also include their original bridal party members from their wedding day, sometimes gathered together in the same room for the first time *since* the original wedding day. This makes a vow renewal celebration a reunion as well, with a sentimental twist as it focuses on your thriving partnership in the past, present, and future.

You had your loved ones at your wedding, and now—at your renewal—your circle of loved ones has grown. Perhaps at your wedding, you mentioned your wish for a family together. Now, your kids and perhaps your grandkids are with you. Your family has grown since then, with new nieces and nephews, your kids' spouses and their families, new friends, clients, colleagues, neighbors . . . the people who have entered and graced your life.

You're planning this event because of gratitude to your spouse, but you soon realize that this celebration is bigger than the two of you. All of these names on your list or in your thoughts right now, in their own ways, played a part in your success story.

Think of the friends and relatives who have been there for you, who helped you through a hard time in your marriage or through a health crisis, a job loss, a move, a difficult life transition. They may have saved the day with their advice and with their thoughtful offers to help. They grieved with you, they laughed with you, and perhaps even taught you through their own examples and deeds. At times, they may have said just the right thing to defuse a simmering fight with your spouse, or they shared the perfect relationship book that guided you both through a period of taking each other for granted. No marriage is an island. Everyone around the couple contributes in some way. Sharing this day with them is a tribute to them as well, when you thank them for all they've added to your life and to your partnership.

Keeping It Small Instead

While it's wonderful to build a big guest list, perhaps doubling the size of your original wedding guest list if you have the desire (and the money), you might feel that you'd much rather share the big day only with your innermost circle. For you, it would be better to just invite your children, your parents, and your closest relatives and friends. A smaller, more intimate group would make it—you imagine—a pure and simple celebration, far cozier and more enjoyable than having to host and mingle with hundreds of guests. Sure, you absolutely do love your three hundred–plus family, friends and colleagues, but this moment is just for you and your closest cohorts.

Here are some examples of why many couples who are currently planning their wedding vow renewal celebrations are keeping the guest list on the smaller size:

- "We don't want a circus. With too many people there, we'd be mingling and moving around the room, catching up with people, talking to everyone . . . and we wouldn't be able to spend quality time with each other."
- "We'd like to invite our kids and our parents as our only guests, which would make it even more special to them to know we consider them our VIPs. We only want to share the moment with them."
- "We really want to have our renewal ceremony at home, so we're

keeping our guest list small so that we can fit people into our living room comfortably."

- "We're keeping it small just to keep our expenses down. Rather than spend so much on a party, we're using the money on our dream second honeymoon!"

Choosing Your "Bridal Party"

Yes, if you'd like, you get to have bridesmaids again! Actually, they'd be called your "attendants," and they can choose from the same selection of stylish designer bridesmaids' dresses on the market as those women preparing to step into the lineup at first-time weddings. Most bridal parties, when given the choice of wearing something they own or buying something new and vibrant for the ceremony will opt for the "something new."

For renewal ceremonies, the roles of bridesmaid and groomsman are purely honorary, a chance for your nearest and dearest to be named an honor attendant and to stand with you as you recite your vows. There are no showers to plan or other traditional roles as found in wedding parties. Groomsmen don't escort guests to their seats (unless that's what you want at a formal celebration), and bridesmaids don't have a mile-long list of things to do (unless they really want to help you out).

Forget the old world rules and expectations that you'll only have one attendant, or that you'll keep your attendants' list small because this isn't a wedding. The rules have broken for first-time brides, so they're broken for you as well. You enjoy the same freedoms now, so you can choose whomever you'd like to stand on both your side and your husband's side. Perhaps you didn't quite have the wedding you wanted when you first married. You may have had a civil wedding with just a few people in attendance, and you always wished you could do it all over again with a bridal party in pink dresses with white and pink bouquets.

Choose as many or as few attendants as you'd like, your same bridal party as at your wedding, or only have your grandchildren in their best party dresses and suits . . . and of course, just the two of you with no attendants at all is also an option.

Your Guest List

Know that guest lists can "get away from you." They can grow and grow to immense proportions when your kids want to invite their dates and friends as well, and your husband comes home with a list of his golf buddies and their wives. Plus, you *really* want to invite everyone in your book club or your work friends who have heard so much about this party from you already. Here again, you're in the same boat as first-time brides with an etiquette issue on your hands. How do you invite some people and not others? Won't family members be insulted if you invite only your closest cousins? How can you not invite all of your work friends? Can you tell your sixteen-year-old daughter that she can't bring her boyfriend of two weeks? Rather than sink into an "it would be easier to just invite the kids" resignation (which always leads to regret . . . which leads to excessive chocolate intake), know that you can handle this. You can be a diplomatic guest list builder who slights no one and includes her top choices.

Here are your steps to taming your guest list:

- First, get a complete list of all possible guests. Your closest relatives and friends, extended family, list them all.
- Now, break down this list into tiers. While the word "tiers" implies a sense of ranking and favoritism . . . well, that's pretty much what you're doing. Your tiers are built according to the groups of people who are most important to you. Your tiers might be: tier 1—the kids, their spouses, and the grandkids; tier 2—our parents, brothers and sisters and their spouses and kids plus grandparents and godparents; tier 3—our best friends (many renewal couples stop right here); tier 4—aunts and uncles we're closest with;

great-aunts and uncles we're closest with; tier 5—our bosses and
closest colleagues; tier 6—cousins we know and like; tier 7—our
kids' friends and their families; tier 8—the neighbors and their
kids; and so on.

- You'll use this tiers list as a way to categorize your guests, so that
you can diplomatically cut groups of them. (That sounds harsh,
but that's the way it goes.) If you're limited on space, knowing
that you can only fit fifty or so people into your house, you'll look
at your tiers list and see that the first six tiers add up to fifty people. So the rest (the kids' friends, the neighbors, etc.) don't make
the list. It's a matter of space.

Hopefully, you come from a family that's not going to give you a
hassle if you invite some but not others. You do, after all, have the
right to invite whomever you wish. If you're approached with a 'why
didn't you invite us?' inquisition from a whiny cousin who didn't even
make tier 12 with you, you can keep your grace and charm by explaining that while you *wish* you could have invited everyone, you simply
didn't have the space.

As it turns out, it's bad etiquette for anyone—*anyone*—to question your choices. You're not the first-time bride, after all. As long as
you and your husband are both happy with your guest list, others will
just have to wait until your *next* renewal celebration or family party or
the family reunion that's coming up next summer.

LADONNA LOGUE KAY AND KENNETH EDWARD KAY, MARRIED FEBRUARY 14, 2003,
RENEWED FEBRUARY 14, 2004

"My husband, Kenny (a Specialist in the North Carolina National Guard), and I planned a large wedding for October 11. We had just put the down payments down on our reception and to our dismay he received deployment papers on Monday, February 10. We were not going to marry before he left. However, at the last minute on Thursday, my husband says to me, 'I just don't want to go over there and God forbid I don't come back and I know that I never got to marry the one person I ever loved.'

"After hearing that, we planned a wedding in twenty-four hours. My husband and I were married at White Dove Wedding Chapel in Wendell, North Carolina, on Valentine's Day 2003. It was a very small chapel with seating for up to thirty people. The most special part of the chapel is that it was originally the Catholic Church that I attended as a small girl. So I was married at the same altar I was baptized at.

"The wedding was a very small ceremony. I was in college at the time so the morning of my wedding I was in school taking an exam. A lot to deal with in one day!

"Kenny was overseas for ten months so we were unable to keep our October 11 bookings. He finally came home in December of 2003 and I called everywhere I knew frantically searching for available dates and miraculously my original chapel, Meredith Chapel at Meredith College in Raleigh, had one day available in an eighteen-month span . . . Valentine's Day! So we planned and planned and were able to renew our vows and have our large ceremony on our one-year anniversary! It was amazing! We have now been married two years just this past February and he is still home safe and sound."

3

SETTING THE STAGE

It's time to set the date. Remember everyone asking you "So when's the big day?" back when you first got engaged to each other? Now, once again, you'll look ahead on your calendar and choose *the* day for your celebration.

You undoubtedly remember from your engaged days that you couldn't set a date until you booked your ceremony and reception locations, and it's the same for you now *if* you'll be holding either of these two sections of your day outside of your home. If you're among the many who hold their renewal events at home or at a friend's or relative's home (more on that in a minute), it's just a matter of picking an open square on the calendar. If you'll renew at your church or synagogue or hold your reception at a restaurant, country club, or estate home—anyplace that requires you to reserve their space and services—you have some work to do before you can set the stage for your renewal celebration.

All three factors—date, time, and place—work together in a synchronicity that adds up to the foundation of your event. You've already sketched out your general wishes earlier in this book, choosing a season or time of day that appeals to you, for instance. Now, use the sections of this chapter to move forward with your planning.

Setting the Date

It could be as simple as "We'll renew our vows on our wedding anniversary," or "How does next Friday work for you?" Setting the date for your renewal ceremony is entirely personal, depending on what works best for you and for the guests you'll invite.

Among couples who renewed their vows, most chose a date that fell on an existing holiday. For most, it *is* the date of their wedding anniversary. As a symbolic day that already calls for a celebration, that's the natural choice. Other popular dates:

Valentine's Day—Does it get more romantic than that? You'll find that renewing your vows on the holiday of love and romance is a gift to both you *and* to your guests when you give them a romantic celebration to enjoy as well.

Thanksgiving—A ready-made family celebration, when everyone's already planning to gather together.

New Year's Eve—Get out the champagne and get ready to party! As the clock counts down to the new year, that's the perfect moment to renew your vows. Everyone gets a little something extra to cheer about, and you get that very special first kiss at midnight.

Christmas or Hanukkah—Again, the family may be gathered, everyone's in a festive mood, the house is decorated beautifully, and you already have fabulous, traditional meals on your menu.

Fourth of July—Take advantage of the town fireworks, especially if you'll renew your vows with a scenic view of a spectacular show over a lake or river.

Holiday weekends, such as Memorial Day or Labor Day, President's Day, etc.—A long weekend could be the perfect time for your family and friends to gather for your special celebration. If you regularly reserve a shore house (or have access to a friend's or relative's shore house), then you can hold your renewal celebration right there on the beach and celebrate throughout the weekend with visits to your favorite restaurants, boat trips, or dinner cruises.

Relationship Renewal Day—May 4 has been designated national Relationship Renewal Day in the card-giving world, so think about this new and growing special day on the calendar.

For the At-Home Celebration

Just a quick note about setting the date when you're holding your entire wedding vow renewal ceremony and celebration at home. Just because it's a home event doesn't always mean any date on the calendar will do. Your key issue is to make sure the date of your event *works*. By that, I mean make sure your home will be available not just on the day of your party but on the days before and after for setup and cleanup. Arrange to have a cleaning service come in to give the place a detailed once-over both before *and* after the party. (Hey, that's a gift in itself!)

Think ahead to the date you have in mind and ask what's going to be going on at your place. Are you planning to redo your kitchen before the big day? Will your garden be in bloom by then? Does it get very muddy in your backyard during the spring rainy season? Choose a date that fits your future home decorating or yard plans and the way you know your property is during the season you have in mind.

You'll find more on hosting at home later in this chapter. We've just dealt with setting a date here . . . there's more to cover as far as considering if your home is the right choice.

WELL, IT'S NOT MY PLACE . . .

Just because it's a home party doesn't always mean it has to be *your* home. A very popular choice is to accept the offer of a friend or relative who suggests that you hold your event in his or her home. It could be that their place is just bigger than yours, or it's an estate with a pool and a gorgeous garden, a beach house, a winter ski house, a bed and breakfast that your friend runs as her business, or maybe your friend has just renovated and redecorated her place and has been looking for the perfect occasion to show it off. Parents may offer their places for your event, excited as they are to host the party for you.

Whoever's place it is, it takes clear communication to set a date that works for both you and for your hosts, and for *their* home and property plans. Sit down with these very generous loved ones and figure out a good three-day block when you can conduct the setup and the cleanup before and after the party. Sometimes hosts aren't aware that they're offering their home for more than one day. Once you choose the dates, offer to get that professional cleaning service for them as well.

How "Wedding World" Affects Setting Your Date

If you're planning "the wedding you never had" and will be booking florists, caterers, five-star hotel ballrooms, and so on, then you'll find yourselves in the same realm as first-time brides and grooms who take nine months to a year to pull their weddings together. Wedding professionals and sites may be fully booked a year in advance. Every weekend may be taken by other couples, especially if you're planning your party for a date within peak season for weddings, May through September. Plan for a good six months to nine months of preparation time, not just to book an available space, but to give *yourselves* plenty of time to plan a big special event without rushing or settling for less than you've dreamed of. Allow yourselves the time to prepare for your big bash, and you'll enjoy the entire process so much more.

Some key points on setting the date:

- Know about the rules for in-season vs. off-season. While you may not be a first-time wedding couple, you're still subject to the pricing and packages of the sites and professionals you approach. During peak wedding season, May through September, hotels' catering and party prices are very likely to be higher per-person, no matter which kind of package you choose. For instance, in the northeast where I live, a cocktail party with sit-down dinner package of five hours might cost $100 per-person in August. Take the *same exact* party with the same exact menu and décor at the same place, move the date to April, and the price could be closer to $50 to $70 per-person. Ask for seasonal price differentials from any site managers or event experts you interview. Those discounts could be very attractive to you, allowing you a much more elaborate party for your budget. In addition, looking at the off-season— like winter months when prices are *really* low due to a lack of demand—you may be able to book a spot sooner than six to nine months from now.
- A date in the off-season has another perk besides time and money . . . you're also not cramming your special event into a summer that's packed with family and friends' weddings, gradua-

tion parties, summer vacations and time-share dates. If you look outside traditional busy times, you'll give your guests (and yourselves) something fun and welcome to look forward to in the off-season. "Everyone *loved* having something fun to look forward to during the dark, dreary winter months. Our February party date gave us all a much-needed lift," says Dawn, who also pointed out that her guests found great travel deals online.

- Match your date to your style. Of course, if you want the outdoor garden party or the beach bash, you'll choose summertime or autumn regardless of whether or not it's peak season. Neither a wait nor a higher pricetag are going to stop you.

- Don't limit yourself to Saturday. In both a budget and a scheduling sense, you'll certainly find great opportunities on a Friday evening or a Sunday afternoon or evening. In the world of catering and special events—or even just if you're booking a party room at a restaurant—these off-days are less in demand, so experts and managers often drop their prices to attract your business. A Sunday night reception could mean 25 to 40 percent less on your total bill.

- Don't limit yourself to the weekend. If you're having a smaller party, and everyone on your guest list lives nearby, then plan your event for a Tuesday night! Your caterer or restaurant manager will be so happy to get an extra reception into the week that you'll receive very attractive pricing. Ask for a consensus on how a workday suits everyone's schedules.

Do You Have the Time?

Setting the time for your renewal is going to depend on your wishes for its style. It could be that your focus is on a sunset renewal of your vows, so you'll choose that as your starting point. Or, it might be that you're sure of the type of *reception* you have in mind. After all, if you want a nighttime dessert and champagne party, you wouldn't set your renewal ceremony for 9:00 a.m. If the celebration is your most vivid image, talk with your officiant (or with your spouse, if you'll be running the ceremony on your own) about the length of the planned *ceremony* that will precede it. Most often, the reception immediately follows the ceremony.

HOW LONG IS THE AVERAGE WEDDING VOW RENEWAL CEREMONY?
In a planning sense, that's up to you. Very few renewal ceremonies are as long as wedding ceremonies. There may not be a High Mass that takes an hour and a half, but rather a short-and-sweet recitation of vows, a reading or two, perhaps a tribute to your kids or parents, and the playing of music. The prevailing average is anywhere from ten minutes to twenty minutes.

Looking at your reception style as the key to planning the time for your event isn't as easy as "dinner is at dinnertime." For you, dinnertime might be 8:00 p.m., while your guests might do dinner at 5:00 p.m. While you've planned a light cocktail party menu for your 6:00 p.m. event, your guests show up expecting dinner and grumbling about the sushi and hot hors d'oeuvres you're serving. Take this kind of expectations difference seriously, as you don't want your guests dialing for a pizza delivery because they're famished.

It's wise for you to use the prevailing timing wisdom from wedding world, matching your celebration to the going etiquette rules about what to plan (and what guests expect) for the time of day:

TYPE OF RECEPTION	TIME OF DAY (START TIME)
Brunch	11:00 a.m.–1:00 p.m.
Luncheon	Noon–2:00 p.m.
Tea	3:00 p.m.–4:00 p.m.
Cocktail Party	4:00 p.m.–7:00 p.m.
Dinner	5:00 p.m.–8:00 p.m.
Champagne and Dessert	8:00 p.m.–10:00 p.m.
"After Hours"	9:00 p.m.–Midnight

The Perfect Location

Your date, time, and place work together like a puzzle. If you have your heart set on a specific date, like your anniversary, then the places you'll consider will have to be available on that day at the time you desire. Or, you know the place you want (the same church and the same restaurant or hotel where you originally held your wedding reception), and so it's the right day and time you have to figure out.

Regardless of when you land here, this section will help you figure out the perfect place to hold your renewal event. Let's start with your ceremony location.

In a House of Worship

Many churches, synagogues and other houses of worship welcome couples to renew their vows. Some allow members or parishioners to schedule their own vow renewal ceremonies in the same way couples might book the house of worship for a wedding, while others plan special services featuring group renewal rites. Another possibility is vow renewal ceremonies offered at the end or as part of a weekend retreat for couples.

Couples who plan to renew their marriage vows in a faith-based ceremony tell me that they appreciate the chance to walk down the same aisles they walked down at their original weddings, that renewing in their own house of worship is a "full circle" experience that adds more meaning. "It just wouldn't be the same in a garden or a restaurant," might be your feeling if you're leaning toward a religious ceremony. You may want the ritual, the rites, the smell of the candles, the blessing of a religious officiant, stained-glass windows. You might want to renew your vows in the church where your parents or grandparents married, especially if you didn't get your wish to do so the first time around.

The religious do-over is a tremendous influence in many couples' decisions to renew their vows. They might have chosen, at the time of their original wedding, to marry in a civil ceremony or in a secular ceremony. Many couples tell me that at their weddings, they "ran into a brick wall" when they tried to reserve a church wedding, with an uninformed or stubborn clerk telling them they could not marry there if they were not recognized members of the church. It happens more often than you'd think. Well, that clerk might not be there anymore, and now you might have a more established standing in the church or synagogue. Your religion has become a larger part of your lives over time, so you'd be stopped by nothing when it comes to finally marrying there.

Another big motivator for the religious ceremony is finding a path later in life. Perhaps you've both evolved in your faith, embraced a new religion, or developed an interfaith plan that's a big part of your relationship. Now, years after your wedding, you have the chance to bring your beliefs into this ceremony as a reflection of who you are at present.

We Did It to Make His Mother Happy—As hard as it might be to admit, perhaps you both married in one church or synagogue just to make a relative happy, to eliminate a simmering family battle. Perhaps his mother, your grandparents, your parents, or an entire side of the family *really* wanted you to marry in the church. Those weren't your strongly held beliefs, but you went along with it for the sake of peace. Now, your do-over allows you to choose the religious setting of *your* wishes.

Or, you married in the church of your faith way back then, with a special dispensation from your husband's house of worship. Now, it's his turn.

Whatever led you to the decision, whether it brings you a sense of rightness or relief, you'll now need to find and reserve the house of worship for your ceremony. Here are the steps you'll follow.

- If you'll book the church or synagogue where you attend, call to make an appointment with the religious officiant to set a date and discuss the elements of your renewal ceremony. Often, you'll find that the house of worship mentions a donation or fee for performing your service, so don't be surprised if there's a dollar sign attached. Sometimes, the fee covers the cost of the staff who prepare the site for your ceremony and clean up afterward.

- If you're not currently a member of any house of worship, but would like to reserve one for your ceremony, then do some research, visit the locations, take tours, and talk to the staff at each. Are you allowed to reserve a ceremony or join in a group service already planned for members? What is required for permission? Do you need to present ID or your marriage license to prove that you're married? (Expect a yes on that one, and get your papers in order.) Most houses of worship will ask for basic facts on your marriage, and some require you to fill out detailed relationship questionnaires in their efforts to guide you and plan your renewal rites. You'll find that many houses of worship have their own rules, and some are more strict than others, that you'll need to obey if you wish to renew there.

Seek and Ye Shall Find

What else do you need to know about a house of worship, besides the fact that it fits your faith, it's *gorgeous*, and you're allowed to renew there? Just a few functional things:

- Is it large enough to seat the people on your guest list? Or do you prefer a smaller space, not a cavernous cathedral, that will dwarf your small guest list?
- Is there air conditioning in summer and heat in winter?
- Is it handicapped accessible?
- Is there parking on-site or nearby?
- Does the site offer use of their choir or musicians?
- Will the site be decorated in any way at the time of your ceremony? (If the site will be decorated for Christmas or Easter, for instance, you won't need to invest in décor.)
- Is the place in good condition? Is it clean and functional?
- Is there plenty of light coming in from windows or is it a darker space?
- Will you be allowed to use candles in your ceremony? (Some houses of worship forbid candles. It's an insurance thing.)
- Will you be allowed to have flash photography? (Some houses of

worship forbid flash photography. It's a "don't hurt the artwork" thing.)

- What are the site's other restrictions? (Some sites won't allow you to bare your head or shoulders, others monitor what you'll say, others do not allow secular music at all.)
- Does the site have a sound system? Not just for the musicians, but for your guests to hear your vows?
- Does the site have a separate room where you'll wait for the ceremony to begin?
- What else do you need to know?

Invest plenty of time in finding the house of worship that feels right to you, that provides just the right mix of solemnity and beauty you desire. Couples write in to tell me about the architecture, the artwork, the amazing pianist, the spectacular orator, the study groups, and the children's programs they've discovered at the houses of worship just a few towns away. Looking for their renewal ceremony site opened new doors to them, which was a perk they didn't expect.

Nonreligious Locations for Your Ceremony

If you don't feel the need to have your renewal ceremony in a house of worship or for a religious officiant, you can renew your vows *anywhere*. All that matters is that you have permission to be there, such as on the grounds of an arboretum, and that there's enough space for all of your guests. Electricity could be a factor for your musicians. Those are the basics as far as functionality. The rest is style. Here are some considerations on what makes for a great ceremony location.

- An amazing view. You might wish to be on the beach or on a terrace overlooking the ocean, perhaps for a sunset vow renewal ceremony. Some couples even plan for sun*rise*, so they can renew on a brand new day. Other views that are in demand: city skyscapes, mountainous overlooks, green forests, winter wonderlands with snowy mountains in the background, an unlimited view of the desert, a clear night sky, a lake with sailboats gliding past.

- Privacy. The beach is your choice, but is it ideal if you're surrounded by drunk spring break–ers? Check the site to see if there's a privacy factor, such as a private beach or landscaping that provides a boundary. At a hotel, a private party room or your own penthouse suite could be the perfect enclosed site (with great views).
- A natural altar, such as a trellis or a bridge spanning a koi pond, a beautiful tree you can stand beneath, a fireplace, a fountain, even a stone grouping, that makes the ideal spot to renew your vows.
- A great approach. Is there a spiral staircase? A marble stairway descending onto the grand lawn of an estate home? A garden pathway? A stone pathway leading right to the beach? Part of your assessment of the perfect location could be the beauty of your entrance surroundings, indoors or out.
- Does it fit your style? A luxurious common room with leather seats and a huge fireplace could be just what you're looking for, not to mention dramatic ceiling beams, chandeliers, and a mahogany bar. Sites like these are found through your historic home association, local tourism board, or chamber of commerce.
- Can you decorate the space? Just like houses of worship, some sites have strict rules about the kinds of décor you can add for your ceremony. They might not want stakes put in the ground for those tiki torches you have in mind, for instance. They might not allow you to bring in any rented plants or to use extra lighting that their power system can't handle. Check on the rules first.
- Will you need a tent and can you put one up? This one is very important, since your dream of an outdoor renewal ceremony could potentially become a washout if a storm passes through. On a functional level, many sites have rules about staking tents into the ground. Some sites will simply not allow it, so you should know that before putting down a deposit on a beautiful, expansive tent for your day. Talk to the site manager about your wishes for

renting a tent, how far in advance you can set it up, what their rules are about putting down flooring for your party. Understandably, an estate home or botanical garden won't want its lawn smothered to death, and you wouldn't want your ceremony plan smothered by an unexpected no.

- What else will you need to rent? Those chairs for your ceremony . . . you might need to rent them. A chuppah? You might need to rent that too. Check www.ararental.org for detailed lists of rental ideas and sources.
- Does it have the required licensing and insurance necessary for parties and gatherings? Always a good thing to ask. You never know.

Unique Locations for Renewal Ceremonies . . . and Receptions

We'd like something different. That's a top request among many renewal couples who don't want to do "the bridal thing" with their celebrations. Instead, they want to express their interests and give their guests a unique experience. Here are the top choices for today's vow renewal ceremonies and celebrations.

- Wineries
- Bed and breakfasts (check www.bbonline.com to find local establishments)
- Dolphin swim parks (such as www.discoverycove.com)
- Butterfly gardens
- Winter festivals (complete with ice sculptures)
- Aquariums
- Private clubs (you'll gain access through a member)
- Alumni clubs (with access to university gardens, party rooms, and ballrooms)
- Estate homes
- Beach homes
- Ski resorts
- Five-star resorts
- Yachts and cruises

- Boardwalks (roller coasters are a big draw for the excitement-inclined, with the carousel popular for the romantics)

Finding the Perfect Place for Your Reception

It could very well be that your ceremony and reception will take place at the same location. For instance, you'll have your ceremony in the rose garden at an estate home, and then the reception in their dining room. At a hotel, your ceremony could take place in a smaller party room (such as the ones used for the cocktail hour at a formal wedding), and then you'll proceed to the ballroom.

That said, use the same criteria you used for your ceremony site (enough space, parking, insurance, a gorgeous view), and add on questions pertaining to the party portion of your event:

- What is the price package for the site?
- How many hours do you get in that package?
- What's the overtime fee if you stay a bit longer?
- Do you need to use their on-site caterers and cake bakers or are you free to bring in your own independently hired team? (Some sites require that you choose from their select list of allowed experts.)
- Is alcohol allowed on the property and grounds? (Check to make sure you can take it outside.)
- Will you need to rent a bar and hire bartenders or does the site provide them?
- Does the site have an ice machine? (More important than you can imagine right now!)
- Is the site's kitchen suitable for your caterer's use? (Bring the caterer in to take a look. Some chefs use oversized baking sheets that don't fit into normal-sized ovens or refrigerators that might be in place at older establishments.)
- Is there a separate area where your caterer will work? (An exposed kitchen isn't sightly.)

- Are you allowed to set up a tent on the grounds? With flooring?
- Do you need permits for gathering, alcohol and food consumption, and food preparation?
- Do you need permits to build a fire or use torches?
- How many restrooms are on the premises?
- Does the site provide tables, chairs, linens, china, and crystal or will you need to rent them?
- What else will you need to rent?
- Is there a separate area you can use for your dessert hour?
- Is there a generator in case of a power failure?
- Is there outdoor lighting for after the sun sets?
- Is there a coat check?
- Is there valet parking or can you arrange for valet parking if you wish?
- Can you arrange for free parking for your guests in the hotel/resort/casino's parking lot or garage?
- Can you get discounted hotel rooms for your guests who wish to stay on-site?

It's a great idea to take notes as you're touring prospective sites, jotting down the answers to these and other questions you think of. Grab a copy of the site's brochure along with the manager's business card too. Take your time, and tour well. The success of your event depends on the time you invest in carefully choosing the perfect environment. Beauty is one thing. A well-run location that sees to the small details is altogether something different. Always look for the signs of a quality establishment, including a site manager or caterer who really listens to you, who treats you like a person, not just a customer to deal with for a fifteen-minute block on a to-do list.

The same rule will apply to the experts you hire for your event, the bakers and florists, limousine company owners, musicians, and others. When they're a quality professional, they'll care as much for your wishes as for their contract.

If you're not treated with respect and interest, walk away. Look for another site. The right one is waiting for you.

Is Your Home the Right Location?

Only you know if your home is the right location for your wedding vow renewal ceremony and celebration. It could feel like the only way you'd want to go. Your home has been the setting for so many of your life's greatest moments, such as bringing your babies home from the hospital, maybe you even gave birth at home. Holidays, family birthdays, anniversary parties . . . your place is the place to be.

If you're on the white-picket fence about the decision and are *considering* it, ask yourself the following questions.

- Consider how you'd like your ceremony to be. Do you imagine walking down the stairs with your husband, standing in front of the bay window with flowers all around you? Or meeting by the pool in the backyard? What's your dream for your at-home celebration?
- Do you have enough space in your home for the size of your guest list? Be honest about the layout of your home. Will people be crammed?
- Do you have enough seating for these guests? You may have to rent chairs, which is not as expensive as you might think.
- Do you have enough china, wineglasses, other glassware, and utensils? Again, you might have to rent these and other important supplies (see Resources).
- Do you have the kitchen space to prepare, refrigerate, and cook food or would you rather cater in? Even if you're catering-in your party, you'll still need refrigerator space to keep foods fresh until serving time and perhaps oven space for reheating.
- Would you worry too much about your white carpet and white couch? Even with the best stain-removing solvent, would you be on edge about spilled red wine? If you treasure your light-colored

furnishings and have tensed up through past family parties, maybe home is not the best choice for you.

- Would you worry about breakables in your home? As a matter of safety, I suggest putting *all* things of value away safely, perhaps in a safe or a lock box, especially at big parties. It's not just your guests who will be in your home, but perhaps serving staff, delivery people, and others. Peace of mind is worth a little bit of neurosis in hiding your bank statements or Lladro figurines.
- Is there enough room for parking on the street outside of your house? In some condo complexes or other limited locations, you get two parking spaces. Everyone else has to park far away and walk. In this case, you can consider hiring a valet service to park cars in a parking lot a few blocks away. Check with your police department or town hall for permits needed for this arrangement.
- Do you have a place to set up a self-serve bar? A dessert table?
- Do you have ample space for guests to put their coats, umbrellas, and boots?
- Do you have a plan for stocking toilet paper and hand towels in the restrooms? (I suggest stocking up an oversized basket and leaving it in each bathroom, rather than assigning someone to toilet paper check duty every hour.)
- Can you ensure privacy for your bedrooms and other personal areas? Can the doors be locked? Or stairs blocked off?
- Can you make arrangements for your housepets? Yes, you know they're friendly, but what if guests are fearful or allergic? If you never lock up the dog, how will you handle this?
- Do you have a plan for kids' entertainment? A separate room with a DVD player and a handful of movies could keep them busy, as could a borrowed Playstation or other game system if there are only a few children on your list.

INSURANCE SMARTS

Partying at home? Check into your homeowner's insurance for the fine print on your liability if a guest falls, gets injured, or gets in a car accident after drinking at your place.

You might need a simple rider added to your existing plan to protect your assets during this and any other gathering at your home or on your property. Talk to your insurance agent for the full details and personalized, informed advice.

JODY BERMAN AND DOAK HEYSER, MARRIED MAY 16, 2004,
RENEWED MAY 16, 2005

"Our renewal 'ceremony' for our first wedding anniversary was quite simple. It was just my husband, Doak Heyser, and myself on a quiet hillside outside of Nederland, Colorado. I got married for the first time at age fifty; Doak was forty-eight—it was his second marriage.

"We started our May anniversary day by brunching at a cafe in the rustic mountain town of Nederland and then drove up the Scenic Peak to Peak Highway. We turned off at the Camp Tahosa Boy Scout Camp and drove a few miles to Beaver Reservoir, a popular trailhead for cross-country skiers. We climbed a hillside with a printed version of our wedding ceremony in tow. Then we proceeded to read together silently the entire ceremony and read aloud our vows to one another. (We wrote the ceremony with help from our 'celebrant,' Noah Saunders, who married us on a magnificent farm.)

"We plan to repeat the private tradition each year but will customize the details of where we will be and what else we might include in our celebration."

4

WHERE IS THE MONEY
COMING FROM?

Some couples do wish to completely avoid the money issue by celebrating out in nature, just the two of them and the words they wish to share. Others, however, are prepared and willing to spend for a lavish party. It's their personal wish to have a big celebration with a cake and entertainment, champagne, a seafood bar, a limousine ride, and other wedding-like treats.

You've heard the statistics about what weddings cost these days. The national average is anywhere from $25,000 to $40,000 depending on where you are in the country. And that's just the national average. Where you live, that could be what brides are spending on their gowns alone. What does this have to do with you? If you're among the many who are planning a vow renewal celebration that *outdoes* the original wedding, you need to know that these are the kinds of figures you'll be facing now in wedding world. Don't panic. There are endless ways to plan your party for less than the national average, so take advantage of the budget ideas in this book. They're designed to help save money for any budget level.

If you're envisioning a smaller scale celebration, rather than a wedding redo, your budget is going to be far less intimidating. You could spend $1,000 total for hors d'oeuvres and drinks, or you could spend $100 on cake and coffee. Your dollar choices are up to you, as you'll plan according to your styles, tastes, wishes, and those extra-special touches you've always dreamed about. Can you get a Vera Wang gown for this event? Absolutely. You can work an extravagance or two into your budget. I'll show you how it's done in this chapter.

Before you start spending your money, you'll need to figure out just how much you'll be devoting to this celebration. Together, the two of you will sit down and agree on a ballpark figure. A nice, round number that gives you the guidance of a limit, yet not a restricting figure. Budgets, as you know, are always flexible. You can go a little bit over or under. Keep track of your own budget expenses throughout your planning process.

Your Priority List

Interested in that Vera Wang gown? Want a really spectacular cake that rivals your wedding cake, rather than the reception to rival your original? Want to get each other amazing renewal gifts or take a second honeymoon rather than throw a big, lavish party? You *can* configure your budget to allow for a grand purchase. All it takes is prioritizing.

Choose the top things that mean the most to you, the ones you're going to devote a larger portion of your budget to. For most first-time brides, 60 percent of their wedding budget goes to their reception, specifically their catering. What will your top choice be? The dress? The menu? Great champagne? A watch for him?

As you head into your planning, you know where you want to spend a little extra. And also where you won't devote as much money.

What's for Free?

If a first-time bride is lucky, she'll get one or two things for free. Maybe the reception hall will throw in the wedding cake for free or maybe she'll get a free bouquet with the purchase of her eight bridesmaids' bouquets. Where are *your* freebies coming from? The use of your house means no site fee. So that's free. Decorating your own convertible for the ride to the reception . . . that means thousands saved on limos. Other areas where renewal couples write a big fat $0 in their budget checklist are:

- Entertainment. It costs nothing to burn your own CDs and play them at your informal party.
- Officiant's fee. If you'll run your own show, you won't be making any donation.
- Photography and videography. Very few renewal couples hire professionals for this event, so you might get the freebie in the form of using your own digital cameras.
- The men's wardrobe. They can wear their own suits (or maybe their own tuxes at this life stage), rather than rent tuxes.
- Your dress? Yes, it's true. Many renewal ladies have chosen to wear a great little black dress they already owned, or something lovely off the rack that costs far less than a wedding gown.
- Cake knife. No dropping $30 on an engraved cake knife. You can use the one from your wedding. The same goes for toasting flutes.
- Whatever people offer to do for you. Knowing that gifts aren't requested or required for your party, guests may bake something or bring something. A relative or friend might offer to make some chocolate-covered strawberries. Another might make your cake. Another could bring a case of wine. Never ask for these items as gifts, of course. Just welcome them as part of your celebration supplies.

Can Hiring a Party Planner Save You Money?

If your celebration will be large, detailed, extravagant, or ultraformal, you might benefit from hiring a professional party planner or special events coordinator. These well-connected pros can save you money by finding you the best experts in the industry and getting discounts. Some coordinators wrangle extra freebies out of the wedding pros with whom they have close working relationships, in exchange for either a flat fee or a percentage of the event's final pricetag if you hire her or him to work your entire event.

You can also hire a wedding coordinator *just* for select tasks, like finding your vendors, negotiating or reviewing your contracts, advising on how many bartenders (or mini-meatballs) you really need, assessing your home for party-readiness, or just showing up on the big day to direct all of the preparations. Check www.bridalassn.com or www.ises.com to find a wedding planner near you, and ask about full versus partial packages that could save you big bucks (and lots of time). Interviewing is key. Be sure you click with a pro and that your wishes are heard and met.

Using the Friends and Family Plan

Of course, you could get great discounts and freebies through your network of friends and family. Think about that friend of yours who works at the beauty salon. Could she arrange for a special deal on a renewal-day manicure and hairstyle? After all, they give first-time brides specially priced packages and champagne breakfasts, right?

Have a friend in the restaurant business? Maybe you could get a nice discount on your dinner or desserts.

Of course, you're not all about the taking. Don't forget the barter system. If you have a skill or trade to barter in equal measure, such as your expertise at designing Web sites, your love of gardening, your baking skills, your genius at writing résumés, offer your return services for any favors asked. Bartering is an often-mentioned strategy used by many of today's renewal couples, with some of their skills including pet-sitting, canning peaches, embroidering handkerchiefs for the recipient to give as gifts to clients, personal shopping, tax advice, and babysitting.

Hiring: Contract Smarts

While I'm sure you're far more experienced at handling contracts and service agreements than when you were first married, you still might find yourself bewildered by some of the business end of today's wedding world. So I'll give you some basic, and some detailed, tips for hiring any experts you'd like to contract for your big day.

- *Always* get a written contract. If any professional says he or she doesn't offer one, walk away. The event industry is big business. You're arranging important and potentially costly events. Always get a detailed contract that spells out your agreements, deposits, final payments due, and initialed changes to any contract language.

- Yes, you can negotiate to make changes to a contract or service agreement. Don't be intimidated by an expert and don't take "that's our contract, no changes allowed" for an answer. As a consumer, you do have the right to request changes.

- Make sure your purchase order is *very* specific. It should mention the exact number, style name, and item code for those things you're buying or renting, exact times and locations of pickups and deliveries, and other specific details so that both you and the provider are clear on what you are getting.

- Always write down the name of the person you spoke to, plus the date and time you talked to them. Keep careful records, including copies of e-mails, in case you need to follow a paper trail if your plans get confused or there's a mistake.

- Always confirm your order with any service providers at least a week before your event. Have them read back your order for extra clarity that they're on the ball.

- Look for hidden fees. Make sure you're aware that a 15 percent gratuity is already added to your purchase so that you don't double tip. Ask to have any corkage fees (that's the money charged for each bottle of wine or champagne the staff uncorks) removed from your bill. The same goes for any cake-slicing fees (the $1.50 to $2.00 charged for cutting each piece of cake for your guests).

- Negotiate out what you don't want. If you're not interested in the international coffee bar during the dessert hour, ask to have that taken out of your plan and off your bill.

- Ask about late fees and overtime fees, with notes made to the contract on exactly when those kick in and the exact dollar amount.

- Ask about refund and cancellation fees, in case you change the date or change your plans. Be sure you're clear on if you can get deposits back, and how you'd go about doing that officially.

- Be sure your professionals are insured. All sites and experts you hire should have their own liability insurance policies. Only work with insured professionals, just to be on the safe side.

TIPPING CHART

One of the most common questions I get pertaining to wedding vow renewals is about the going rate for tipping experts. Even though your event may be small and less formal than your original wedding, it's still a must to tip your experts well. The following amounts are merely guiding suggestions; you're free to give more to professionals who exceeded your expectations and really made your day special.

- Event planner: 10 to 20 percent of your bill, depending on the terms of contract
- Officiants: $50 to $100
- Ceremony site staff: $20 to $30 per person
- Organists and ceremony musicians: $20 to $40, depending on length of service
- Reception site manager: 15 to 20 percent of entire bill for the reception
- Valets: $1 per car
- Waiters: $20 to $40 each, depending upon quality of service
- Bartenders: 15 percent of liquor bill
- Coat check: $1 per coat
- Limousine drivers: 15 to 20 percent of transportation bill (Check to see if tip is already included in the contract first! If so, then on-the-day tip may be smaller as a token for great service.)
- Photographer and videographer: $20 to $100 or more
- Delivery workers: $10 each if just dropping items off, $20 each if dropping off and setting up to a great extent; more so if they're transporting a LOT of items
- Tent assemblers and rental agency assemblers: $20 each, more so if the tent is extremely large or complicated, or parquet flooring is set down as well
- Entertainers: $25 to $30 each, more if they really exceeded expectations

- Beauticians and barbers, manicurists and makeup artists: 15 to 20 percent of beauty salon bill
- Cleanup crew: $20 each
- Babysitters: $30 to $40 each, plus a gift, in addition to their hourly wages; more if baby-sitter is putting in extra hours or caring for several children

Part 2

PLANNING THE CEREMONY

JULIO AND AGUEDO BREZO, MARRIED JANUARY 18, 1959,
RENEWED FEBRUARY 5, 1984

"Both our original wedding in Cuba in 1959 and our wedding vow renewal
in Miami in 1984 were presided over in Catholic churches by the same
priest, the Reverend Father Armando Balado, who also immigrated to the
United States as we did. He conducted our ceremony in Spanish, just as we
did the first time. About one hundred people attended our renewal, including many of the same guests who were at our original wedding, and now
joined us with their families. We had a slide show featuring our wedding
photos, which was very touching, since many of our relatives had since
passed on."

5

WHO RUNS YOUR
CEREMONY?

Who will stand before you and lead your ceremony? Who will read the words you will repeat to one another or perform a sermon or ritual? It's your choice. Unlike wedding couples, your ceremony doesn't need to be validated by a state-recognized officiant to seal your vows in the eyes of the law. You've already done that, so the leader of your reaffirmation ceremony may be anyone you wish.

A Religious Officiant
It could be the priest, minister, or rabbi who originally conducted your wedding, now conducting your vow renewal ceremony, a personalized and meaningful touch that so many couples say added the perfect "full circle" element to their day. Particularly if you still have a close relationship with this officiant, it could mean the world to you to have him or her guiding you now.

If you do not have access to the original religious officiant who married you, you can certainly interview religious leaders of your choice. If you're new to a house of worship, this would be a terrific opportunity for you to meet with the inhouse officiant for a discussion on your renewal wishes and perhaps additional information on how you both can get more involved in your faith. This type of unexpected advantage is so often mentioned as a meaningful benefit to renewing vows.

Another option that's hot right now is joining together two different religious leaders in a custom-blended, multifaith ceremony that joins both of your belief systems into your beautifully personalized ceremony. As mentioned earlier, perhaps you had to choose just one faith for your wedding, with one partner's religious affiliation put aside (with or without outside pressure). Now, you've both changed and grown over the years, as your faith balance may have, so bringing in separate officiants for proper homage to both your shared and individual beliefs is the ideal way to celebrate the faith-based tapestry of your marriage. You may not have had the option to do so back then, but you may certainly do so now.

Where do you find an officiant? Check the Web sites of your local churches or synagogues, where you may find a link to their vow renewal guidelines. Check religious association Web sites (see Resources) for direct referrals to religious leaders and houses of worship in your area. And talk to friends and family who have lasting relationships with their houses of worship for those oh-so-valuable personal referrals and suggestions.

Religion–Lite?

You may want a religious or spiritual angle to your renewal ceremony, but not quite enough to lead you into the world of strict religious requirements. Your choices are "softer," as your beliefs may be a conglomeration of religion and spirituality. It might be your experience that some religious officiants are less flexible in what they'll grant for your ceremony. Again, this is a purely case-by-case basis, and while couples who do take this route may call it "religion *lite*," it could be the ideal reflection of how your relationship has grown under a more relaxed version of your views on faith. As you search, you'll look for officiants in perhaps another branch of religion. Couples tell me that their own personal search led them to believe that the Unitarian or Presbyterian or Baptist churches near them seemed more inviting to personalized vow renewal ceremonies. I cannot make pronouncements, of course, on which church to go to, but I can let you know that thousands of couples across the country did venture to explore different denominations with not an ounce of their faith reduced. For them, this path allowed them to celebrate their beliefs more fully and realistically, and often found them a religious community that became a larger part of their lives after the big day.

Independent Ministers and Officiants

Nondenominational officiants, independent ministers, and others who stand beneath an umbrella of personalized praise are a hot ticket for today's wedding vow renewal couples. "We want a faith angle, but also more of a spiritual angle," some couples tell me. Or "We couldn't find a priest who would allow us the kinds of irreverent and funny elements we wanted in our ceremony." Overall, couples who seek out independent or nondenominational officiants would like authorship over their ceremonies, with the guiding hand of an open and perhaps spiritual advisor. This may be the best reflection of how they live their lives and belief systems.

TALKING TO AN OFFICIANT

Rev. Laurie Sue Brockway, an ordained interfaith minister and nondenominational wedding officiant in New York City (www.RevLaurieSue.com) says, "There are a number of reasons that couples today are seeking nontraditional officiants, many of whom have their own wedding ministry, independent from a larger religious institution." These include:

- "Many couples are seeking 'spirit' without necessarily having religion in their ceremony."
- "Many couples want a very personalized ceremony and not all traditional clergy are willing to allow a couple to put their special touch on a ceremony."
- "When it comes to vow renewals . . . most couples do not really want to repeat what they did in the past, but would like a new ceremony that builds on the years they have been together and honors the place they have come to together. They want a ceremony that celebrates their love, and strengthens their bond. It has to be personal, and meant for them only. That's why they may seek a nontraditional officiant, or even have a trusted friend or family member preside."

If you wish to locate and interview independent officiants for your renewal ceremony, visit www.WeddingOfficiants.com for a complete list of accredited leaders in your area.

Spiritual and Cultural Advisors

Since the choice of officiant is up to you, you might opt for a more spiritual officiant whose ceremonies you know and adore. Many couples have written in about their nature-based spiritual leaders, Native American leaders, or solstice ceremonies conducted artfully and musically by a recognized speaker or elder in a spiritual order. If the two of you embrace a more spiritual path, or belong to a specialized spiritual group, your leader could be chosen from this realm. I *don't* suggest just opening the phone book and calling a spiritual officiant cold from the Yellow Pages. Couples who sheepishly admit doing this have some great cocktail party stories to share: anyone can call themselves a spiritual officiant and buy an ad in the paper. Trust me . . . interview all of your potential officiants.

Secular Leaders

Just as wedding couples do, you could arrange for the mayor to conduct your ceremony, or a justice of the peace or judge. A secular officiant may bring you back to your wedding day when the mayor married you in a park or on your parents' front lawn. Couples who choose a secular officiant for their renewal ceremony say that the religious aspect wasn't for them, that faith doesn't play a strong role in their relationship, so it would seem false to bring religion into their ceremonies. Or that picking one partner's religious beliefs over another's would cause hurt feelings or cause a maelstrom of confusion when the one couple subscribes to multiple religious beliefs. A Catholic–Jewish–Kabbalah–Native American mysticism ceremony would just be too much for what they've planned as a simple ceremony based only on their vows.

Someone You Know

Since this isn't a wedding where the officiant has to be licensed to perform ceremonies, you can ask a friend, a daughter or son, a parent, a relative, the couple who introduced you originally, your godparents, or the funniest guy you know to serve as your officiant and lead your vow renewal ceremony. This adds another element of personalization and deeper meaning to your day, when a person close to you takes a position of honor in guiding your vow renewals. He or she can give a short speech, recite a reading, introduce you and other honored guests, announce song performances, explain rituals, and, most important, invite you to renew your vows to one another. Couples say they love to have their children lead the ceremony, as a pair or as a group, each child reading from a script and gaining the wonderful feeling of "doing something important" for their mom and dad.

It's All You

You might choose not to have an officiant at all, but rather run the ceremony on your own, as a couple. You know what you want to say, and you don't need any guidance. You'll speak your words, renew your vows, and pay tribute to your kids, your families, and friends exactly the way you wish. You don't need to search for a priest, a minister, or a Native American shaman to lead you.

Questions to Ask Potential Officiants

These questions apply to *all* of your options, from the priest or rabbi to the independent minister, interfaith officiants, priestesses, shamans, and some of the questions apply to your kids. This *is* an honored position with responsibilities, after all, so as a matter of business or just pure crossing all the T's for your own organizational peace of mind, ask the following questions of the officiants who may be in charge of your ceremony:

- Do you perform vow renewal ceremonies?
- How many ceremonies have you performed?
- Have you performed ceremonies in the style and theme we have in mind?
- What will you wear to the renewal ceremony? (This question was suggested by a couple whose officiant showed up in a neon purple robe with orange sash and crown of feathers.)

- Do you need any paperwork from us? (Religious and interfaith officiants, or others, will likely want to see some ID and perhaps your marriage license to be sure you're really married.)
- What are your fees?
- Do you have time minimums or maximums, and what are your overtime fees?
- Do you charge for travel?
- Do you have sample scripts and readings that we can review?
- Can we see photos and testimonials from other renewal ceremonies you've run?
- Do you have video or DVD footage of ceremonies you've run, and can we review them?
- Do you perform the spiritual or cultural rites we have in mind?
- Would you be willing to learn and incorporate our requested rituals into the service? (Some might not be willing to enact a ritual with which they're not familiar.)
- Will you be willing to help us write the service?
- Will you be willing to review our service script ahead of time?
- Do you have any locational issues, such as not performing ceremonies outdoors? (Some do not want to face the elements.)
- Will we get a certificate or scroll commemorating our vow renewal ceremony?

Since your ceremony will be personalized, write down any other questions you'd like to ask of your potential officiants.

_____

_____

_____

_____

_____

Watch the Vibe

When you meet with any officiant—and *always* meet with them; never do an interview over the phone or make a decision based on a pretty Web site—take some time to notice his or her rapport with you, the vibe you get from them. Do they speak clearly or in an off-putting way, perhaps rambling or mumbling or at a rapid-fire pace? Do they take the time to listen? Do you feel comfortable and welcome with this person? Can you see this person leading your ceremony? It's a matter of the right fit, so be sure this officiant answers your questions fully and shows that they understand and value your requests.

ANDREA AND RON OBSTON'S THIRTIETH, MARRIED JUNE 25, 1972,

RENEWED EVERY FIVE YEARS, ON OR ABOUT JUNE 25

Andrea and Ron have renewed their vows every five years. They're both writers and here are the vows from their most current celebration at the Norwich Inn and Spa.

Greeting

RON: *We thank you for accepting our invitation to join us today, as we renew our vows.*

ANDREA: *It's a special day, because thirty years ago, on a rainy Sunday, Ron and I came together with our friends and families to promise our lives to one another. Some of those present then are not able to be here, but we know they are with us in spirit.*

RON: *Since that day thirty years ago, we've learned more about life and love.*

ANDREA: *Sometimes we're lovers and friends.*

RON: *Sometimes we're brother and sister.*

ANDREA: *We've fought and made love and added one superior human being to the face of the earth through our love.*

RON: *We've laughed and cried.*

ANDREA: *But always our love grows, and today, we want to renew the vows we gave to each other thirty years ago.*

Ceremony

BOTH: *Coming nearer to the one I love, our pathways merge in the garden.*

ANDREA: *We come to be closer to God.*

BOTH: *We come to experience life.*

BOTH: *We come to be partners in love.*

Vows

RON: *I will love you forever.*

ANDREA: *I will love you freely and purely.*

RON: *We will hold hands and together grow.*

ANDREA: *We will embrace with passion.*

BOTH: *We will give ourselves. We will journey as one. We will be companions for all time.*

Rings

BOTH: *These wedding bands are like our love.*

RON: *Two gold strands intertwined.*

ANDREA: *Two people joined in life.*

BOTH: *So with these rings, we bind ourselves in love.*

(Andrea and Ron then shared a cup of wine in a toast to their guests.)

BOTH: *Where our paths become one trail of joy and our journey the way of love. Where a kiss of the sun is for pardon and the song of the birds is for mirth. We come nearer to God's heart in the garden than anywhere else on earth.*

6

THE PERFECT WORDS

Your vow renewal ceremony is all about the perfect words. While it's exciting to plan a gathering with friends and family, create your bouquet and plan a delectable menu, perhaps arrange a destination event on a tropical island, the basis of the entire event is the renewing of your marriage commitment. What will you say to one another? What are the expressions in your heart? Can you put that feeling, that indescribable peace and gratitude for one another and the life you've shared, into words the way you'd like? Of course. The perfect words for you both are yours to create. They're a gift you give to one another, more lasting than anything that can be wrapped and tied with a bow (or worn on your finger). Even better, the words you speak are a gift *to those around you*. They too absorb the love in what you say, and they too remember your expressions.

So many husbands and wives tell me that they realized they don't say "I love you" often enough to their partners . . . and these are the happy couples with great partnerships. Wives wish their husbands would be more expressive; husbands wish they were better at expressing what they're feeling. It's a common thing. Love letters are cherished for what they express, and even if Hallmark has done the work of crafting the actual sentences, the gift from spouse to spouse has lasting meaning and soldifies their relationship. Who doesn't love to get a romantic card or a love letter? Whose relationship isn't strengthened by a regular compliment or an "I love you"? This is the lesson for couples who are renewing their vows: a reminder to speak loving words more often, to validate and value each other outwardly, not just at a renewal ceremony, but as often as possible in their every shared day and night.

In this chapter, you'll take on the important and meaningful task of crafting the words you'll speak during your vow renewal ceremony. Before you write a thing, though, consider the most common *styles* of vow renewal wording.

Repeating Your Original Vows—For many couples, it's even more meaningful now to repeat the exact same words they spoke at their wedding ceremonies. *For better or for worse, for richer or for poorer, in sickness and in health, forsaking all others* . . . You have a history of doing just that, and speaking these same promises to one another reseals the foundation of your marriage. You'd like to keep it pure, so you'll repeat the same vows exactly, whether they were the traditional church script or the original vows you wrote for each other on your own. That's what means the most to you, turning the vow moment from your wedding into a *twice* in a lifetime blessing.

Repeating Your Original Vows, with a Little Something Extra—You'll repeat your original vows, exactly as you both said them on your wedding day, and then pay tribute to the marriage you've shared since that moment with an add-on expression at the end. For instance, you might then go on to say, "The past fifteen years have been an adventure, a comfort, a gift. You become more of a best friend to me each and every day, and I'm so grateful to you for all that you do, for all that we'll share in the future, and for the things that I've learned and continue to learn from you every day. I offer you my heart now and onward in the future as your loving and faithful partner. I still do love, honor and cherish you, and I always will." The "something extra" can be shared vows you'll both repeat, as you've written them together as a team, or you could surprise each other with what you've each written on your own.

This Time, You'll Get to Say What You Wanted to Say Then—At the time of your wedding perhaps your house of worship required that you repeat their standard vows script. There was no negotiation, no customizing, no taking out the word "obey." You were young, or you hadn't found your voice or assertiveness yet, so you agreed to repeat those traditional vows. Now, you'll get to alter them or create entirely new ones. You're not limited by any rules or requirements, so you own creative control over your wording. Finally. It's a do-over, a deeply meaningful wish you've always carried with you: that you could say what's in your heart instead of what's on an index card. Many couples tell me that they've grown more religious over time (or more spiritual or more naturalist) and that the vows they speak today reflect who they are now, both individually and as a couple. Redoing their vows is a chance to speak as the person they've grown into . . . making this ceremony even more personal for them both.

Building Your Vows on a Song—You might use the lyrics of "your" song as the foundation for your vows or just a phrase from a song that captures what's in your heart to springboard your expressions of love and commitment. Some popular songs at vow renewal ceremonies are "Just the Way You Are" by Billy Joel, "Our Love Is Here to Stay" by Nat King Cole, "The Way You Look Tonight" by Fred Astaire, "Evergreen" by Barbra Streisand, "Still the One" by Shania Twain, "Endless Love" by Luther Vandross and Mariah Carey, "Amazed" by Lonestar, "Just You and I" by Eddie Rabbitt and Crystal Gayle, "Always and Forever" by Heatwave, and "All of Me" by Louis Armstrong. Also by Louis Armstrong, the top pick among many couples: "What a Wonderful World."

FINDING SONG LYRICS

Browse through a collection of great songs, looking for your song or another song that reflects the depth of your relationship now (thereby claiming a new song for your future together) at the following lyrics Web sites.

www.lyricsdepot.com

www.lyricsfreak.com

www.romantic-lyrics.com

www.sing365.com

Building Your Vows on a Quote—"Grow old along with me, the best is yet to be" from a Robert Browning poem is among the most popular classic quotes used in wedding ceremonies, and may be the perfect start to your vow renewal. Poetry and great quotes have long been a staple of wedding vows and speeches. They've graced the front covers of wedding programs and brought into your world the immortal thoughts of poets like Shakespeare, Elizabeth Barrett Browning, John Keats, and Maya Angelou, or spiritual writers like Don Miguel Ruiz, Marianne Williamson, Anne Morrow Lindbergh, and Wayne Dyer, or philosophers like Emerson and Lao Tzu. You might choose a romantic quote, a spiritual one, a funny one, or the quote that originally brought you two together, the one that opened a great discussion on your first date.

FIND QUOTES FOR YOUR VOWS

Browse the following quote Web sites, in addition to romantic quote books you'll find in the bookstore or library, for a wealth of quote possibilities to use now and in the future.

www.romantic-lyrics.com

www.weddingchannel.com

www.brainyquotes.com

www.quotemeonit.com

Quotes to Consider

I've collected just a small sampling of the most popular quotes used in today's wedding vow renewal ceremonies.

Whoso loves believes the impossible.

—ELIZABETH BARRETT BROWNING

In dreams and in love, there are no impossibilities.

—JÁNOS ARANY

Those alone are wise who know how to love.

—SENECA

If you would marry wisely, marry your equal.

—OVID

I am, in every thought of my heart, yours.

—WOODROW WILSON

Love indeed is a light from heaven a spark of that immortal fire.

—GEORGE GORDON, LORD BYRON

The journey is always towards the other soul.

—D. H. LAWRENCE

Words of love are works of love.

—W. R. ALGER

It is love that asks, that seeks, that knocks, that finds, and is faithful to what it finds.

—ST. AUGUSTINE

Blessed is the influence of one true, loving human soul on another.

—GEORGE ELIOT

My fair one, let us swear an eternal friendship.

—JEAN BAPTISTE MOLIÈRE

She gets into the remotest recesses of my heart and shines all through me.

—NATHANIEL HAWTHORNE

Whatever our souls are made of, his and mine are the same.

—EMILY BRONTË

How vast a memory has love!

—ALEXANDER POPE

You were made perfectly to be loved—and surely I have loved you,
in the idea of you, my whole life long.
— ELIZABETH BARRETT BROWNING

I never knew how to worship until I knew how to love.
— HENRY WARD BEECHER

Heaven will be no heaven to me if I do not meet my wife there.
— ANDREW JACKSON

To get the full value of joy, you must have someone to divide it with.
— MARK TWAIN

If I know what love is, it is because of you.
— HERMANN HESSE

Love doesn't make the world go round,
Love is what makes the ride worthwhile.
— ELIZABETH BARRETT BROWNING

Being deeply loved by someone gives you strength,
While loving someone deeply gives you courage.
— LAO TZU

What lies behind us, and what lies before us are tiny matters
compared to what lies within us.
— RALPH WALDO EMERSON

I love thee, I love but thee
With a love that shall not die
Till the sun grows cold
And the stars grow old.
— WILLIAM SHAKESPEARE

One word frees us of all the weight and pain in life,
That word is Love.
— SOCRATES

And think not you can
direct the course of love,
For love,
if it finds you worthy,
directs your course.
— KAHLIL GIBRAN

Smile at each other, smile at your wife,
smile at your husband, smile at your children,
smile at each other—it doesn't matter who it is—
and that will help you to grow up in greater love
for each other.
— MOTHER TERESA

Love does not consist in gazing at each other
but in looking together in the same direction.
— ANTOINE DE SAINT-EXUPÉRY

Readings

THE MOST POPULAR READING AT VOW RENEWAL CEREMONIES

Love is patient, love is kind. It does not envy, it does not boast, it is not proud. It is not rude, it is not self-seeking, it is not easily angered, it keeps no record of wrongs. Love does not delight in evil but rejoices with the truth. It always protects, always trusts, always hopes, always perseveres.

—1 Corinthians 13:4–7

In addition to quotes, you may also choose to include the same readings that you had at your wedding ceremony or new ones. Consider your favorite scripture passages, or lines from a spiritual book, even an inspiring section of a novel . . . anything that speaks to the meaning of the day. While the most popular reading at vow renewal ceremonies, as mentioned here, is Corinthians 13, here are others for you to consider.

> *What greater thing is there for two human souls than to feel that they are joined for life, to strengthen each other in all labor, to rest on each other in sorrow, to minister to each other in all pain, to be with each other in silent, unspeakable memories at the moment of last parting.*
>
> —GEORGE SAND

> *From the beginning, God made them male and female. For this cause shall a man leave his father and mother, and cleave to his wife; they shall be one flesh; so then they are no more twain but one flesh. What therefore God hath joined together, let not man put asunder.*
>
> —MARK 10:6–9

> *Love is not love*
> *Which alters when it alteration finds.*
> *Or bends with the remover to remove.*
> *O no! It is an ever-fixèd mark,*
> *That looks on tempests and is never shaken.*
> *It is the star to every wandering bark,*
> *Whose worth's unknown, although his height be taken.*
>
> —WILLIAM SHAKESPEARE

> *Oh, the comfort, the inexpressible comfort of feeling safe with a person; having neither to weigh thoughts nor measure words, but to pour them all out, just as they are, chaff and grain together, know-*

*ing that a faithful hand will take and sift them, keep what is worth
keeping, and then with the breath of kindness, blow the rest away.*
— GEORGE ELIOT

Designing Your Ceremony

When you plan your ceremony—which is indeed the most important
part of your day—you'll go step by step through the elements you desire, such as *Processional, Greetings, Blessing of the Congregation, Readings, Musical Interlude, Reading of Vows, Exchanging of Rings,* and
Recessional.

Most couples look back at their original wedding programs for
guidance, sometimes adding a musical interlude, and they'll once
again print up programs to hand out to guests, complete with a personal thank you message from the two of them.

Following your wished-for ceremony outline, the officiant will
read either a script that he or she often uses for renewal services—
you'll select from the provided repertoire or portfolio of options—or
from a script that you've custom written for your relationship, your
challenges, your wishes. You have both options open to you.

Here are some examples of officiant-led renewal scripts.

The Opening: Before the Vows

David and Jennifer, you stand here before us all with the
intention of renewing your wedding vows. You serve as an
example of all that is real about marriage, the challenges and
opportunities for growth, the fine times and the darker days
that you've passed through hand-in-hand, in triumph or in
tears, always holding on to one another with value and respect,
laughter and pride. You've created a beautiful family that looks
to you each day for guidance and with reverence. You are the
center of your children's lives, as well as the center of each
other's lives. It is my honor to participate in this service as you

reaffirm your commitment to one another. Will you please repeat after me . . .

The officiant then reads the couples' original wedding vows, pausing between phrases for husband and wife to repeat their vows.

Or,

Kelly and Thomas, as you prepare to renew your wedding vows and enrich your commitment to one another, take a moment to think about the road you've traveled together thus far. Think about the many experiences you've shared, the people who have come into your lives, the seasons through which you've passed . . . this is the future you hoped for on your wedding day.

Be thankful for the past and then release it with gratitude.

This is a new beginning for you both, a renewal not just of your vows but of your relationship and your life together.

Whatever challenges you faced, you're free of them now. The challenges that are to come have no chance against the strength of your bond. I'll lead you now through the same vows you spoke on your wedding day.

Vows You'll Speak to Each Other

After your processional and greeting, you will recite your vows. You might stick to your own script or venture off to include a new sentiment that's just occurred to you. Spontaneous emotion is always a welcome guest at a vow renewal ceremony, so if a heartfelt thought has popped into your mind, feel free to enhance your planned speech and include it. There can be no greater personalization.

How detailed can you get? That's up to you. Most couples keep it simple, short and sweet, needing no embellishments but rather just the purity of their promises to one another. Consider the traditional vow renewal script, which borrows from traditional wedding vows:

I, [name], take you, [name],
my [husband/wife],
to have and to hold,
from this day forward,
for better or for worse,
for richer or for poorer,
in sickness and in health,
to love and to cherish,
'til death do us part.
According to God's holy law
and covenant.
This is my solemn vow.

Or, you could personalize your vows completely, sounding more like you than like a formal script:

Michael, you have given me the "happily ever after" I dreamed of on our wedding day. Every day, I say a little prayer of thanks that I have been so blessed as to share my life with you. You remind me every day that there is no limit to the amount of joy one person can bring another. I promise you now, still and always that I do love you . . . and always will.

Patricia, words cannot do justice to the feeling I have in my heart right now. You are the most beautiful woman I've ever known. The day you said yes to me was the happiest day of my young life, and each day I get to wake up next to you is the happiest day of my present life. I will always love you, will always spend my days making you feel as treasured as you have made me feel.

What Can You Promise at This Point?
I still do . . .

It can be the opener of all that you've promised before, all you've promised throughout your partnership on real-life days when the kids have the flu, the dog needs to go to the vet, work deadlines loom, and your in-laws are coming for the weekend. Now, with a formal celebration, you might be thinking that the unspoken promises you've lived by, that have become second nature to you, can't quite easily make their way into words. What can you promise to one another now . . . when you've been living the promises?

Think about what you'd like to give a recharge to. What in your relationship is there, but in black-and-white rather than in color? Does anything need a freshening? Not CPR, as in the case of a marriage in trouble, but a brush-up like restoring a painting or picture to bring out brighter colors, clearer images, more detail. Has anything grown foggy in the image of your life together? Here is where you'll record *the new things* you'd like to promise one another. I've started with a few suggestions and left room for your own musings:

- I will embrace the moment you come home, not race through the moment and forget what a gift and a comfort it is to hear your key in the door lock . . .
- I will remember each day that it's not a to-do list that matters, but who I'm doing it for . . .
- I will not just remember the words you say, but thank you for them . . .
- I will treasure your character . . . the honesty when it's hard to be honest with me sometimes, your generosity of spirit when it's a challenge to get me to accept what you offer, your lightness of heart when I'm taking myself too seriously . . .

Blessing of the Rings

At this point, after your vows are spoken, you may choose to exchange your rings as a symbol of your commitment, once again hearkening back to your wedding day. They may be your original rings, upgraded versions, or surprise upgrades that you'll read about later in this book. Whatever the carat-count, the wording you plan for this very important element of your renewal ceremony is a gift in itself.

Spoken by the Officiant

Let these rings be a symbol of everlasting faithfulness between this man and this woman, a symbol of the vows that they have taken in the past, have lived each day in whole and pure partnership, and will continue to believe in and cherish forever into the future. Bless these rings and the husband and wife who wear them as they repeat after me . . . [Name], I give you this ring as a token of my continued affection, as a sign of our marriage, and as a symbol of our everlasting union. All that I am, I give to you. With all that I have, I honor you. And with all that I will be, I share my life with you.

Or,

The ring is a symbol of eternity which this man and this woman have pledged to one another their solemn vows and heartfelt offerings of eternal love and loyalty. The circle is never ending. There is no marker where it ends and where it begins. So is the love between this husband and this wife. As you place these rings upon one another's fingers, please recite your vows to one another.

Spoken by the Two of You

I give you this ring once again as a reminder of the eternal commitment we have made to one another, the commitment we live by every day, the commitment we celebrate today.

Or,

I give you this ring as a token of my love, my loyalty, my appreciation for all that you have been to me and to our children for the past [number of] years. Seeing this ring on your hand is a daily reminder to me of just how lucky I am to have you and call you mine.

Bringing In a Ritual

The words you speak might be tied to a ritual that symbolizes your union. It might be a traditional sake or tea ceremony, which Asian custom symbolizes meeting the partner's needs before your own as you fill another's cup and present a sip to the honored party. In wedding rituals, this ceremony is often conducted between families, with the bride offering her prospective in-laws a cup of tea in an elaborate ritual that's packed with meaning, respect, and generations' worth of practice.

You might bring in the Eastern European ritual of presenting one another with bread, wine, and salt to symbolize the building blocks of a fortunate life. The exchange of food is a long-standing ritual in uniting ceremonies like these, either with a taste or an offering to each other. Look into your heritage, into your cultures to see which food or drink rituals could be the perfect accent and enhancement to your renewal ceremony. You might discover a beautiful rite that you can include now, and then *start a new anniversary ritual with*, such as offering one another bread and wine at the start of your anniversary dinner each year in the future. Your renewal, then, becomes the beginning of a new practice to further unite you.

Another popular wedding and renewal ritual is *handfasting*, in which the husband and wife's hands are bound together by a cord, a rosary, or a prayer shawl, any symbolic item that can be used to tie your hands together. You'll either be holding hands when the cord is tied or your hands will be pressed together in a prayer formation. Your officiant will share the meaning of the ritual, which is to symbolize your bond, and leave the cord in place while speaking through the ceremony. You might have had a handfasting ritual, or have carried your rosary wrapped around your hands, at your wedding ceremony, so this is a wonderful way to bring the same element into your present.

One new twist that renewal couples are choosing is to have their *children* untie the cord at the end of the ceremony (so that they may exchange their rings), rather than have the officiant proclaim them forever bound and release the cord. Asking a child or a parent to untie the cord is an honor akin to lighting the unity candle.

The unity candle is another ritual that's also growing in popularity for the vow renewal couple. They might bring their original wedding unity candle out of storage to light once again in the same church where they were married, or in their home, or wherever their ceremony takes place. Or, if they did not have a unity candle at their wedding, they might buy a beautiful one now for this ceremony. Just as at weddings, the unity candle is lit by both the husband and the wife to symbolize the light of their partnership. It might be lit as music is playing or before they speak their vows or during a reading by the officiant as he or she explains the symbolism to the guests: "As husband and wife, you will now light the unity candle, which is a symbol of the light that shines from you both, reflecting on all who look upon you."

The words you speak, or have spoken for you, could tie in a myriad of symbolic statements:

- Together, you've kept the flame of your marriage lit.
- The light of your partnership gives you direction, warmth, and comfort on your journey together.
- Each day, a renewal, like the renewal of the flame on our wedding unity candle.

Another ritual you might enact is to have your children light their own candles and place them around yours before you light your unity candle. All of these candles become part of the ceremony, and are then taken home for use in future family rituals. Perhaps becoming your children's future wedding candles as well.

Sharing the Love with Your Guests

As part of your renewal ceremony, you might choose to share the joy with all of your married or committed guests, including your kids. As a surprise to them, you or your officiant might turn at the conclusion of your renewal to invite *them* to do the same. They might be invited to repeat a blessing to one another, a reading, or a simple vow such as "I still do." Some couples hand out roses to the gentlemen among their guests with a note saying "Stay tuned . . ." and at this point, the men would be invited to give the roses to their wives, girlfriends, fiancées, or partners. It's a nice touch, a way to allow your loved ones the chance to have a special moment of their own.

Taking Vows with Your Children

At the conclusion of your ceremony, or during it, you might wish to take vows as parents, speaking words of love and appreciation to your children. Your kids may be infants, small children, teens, or adults; at any age, they can be honored as the special part of your relationship that they are, for all they bring to your lives, for the family they are to you. You might speak words to them as a group or to each of them individually, thanking them each for the gifts they bring to you and to the family as a whole. You might give them a gift or a long-stemmed rose or hand them a card with a private message from the two of you in addition to the public declarations you've just made. You might play a song for your entire family, as a recessional that you'll all enact hand in hand as a group. You've walked down the aisle as a couple, and now you'll walk back up the aisle as a family.

JOANNE AND ANDREW BLAHITKA, MARRIED MAY 22, 1965,
RENEWED MAY 22, 2005

"For our fortieth wedding anniversary, we wanted to take a moment
together for a toast. It had been a very trying year for us. I'd undergone
chemotherapy for non-Hodgkins lymphoma for most of the year, went into
remission, then had a setback. I was hospitalized for three weeks, most of
them in intensive care, due to pneumonia and a stomach infection. The
entire family went through quite a trauma with that, and my daughters and
son devoted the majority of their year to my care and to keeping up my
house while running their own lives as best they could. So at the time of our
wedding anniversary, we wanted to keep our renewal ceremony very quiet
and low-key, just a simple toast and a nice dinner at home with our kids.
Then we went outside and planted a new peony plant right next to my departed mother's peony plant, which has been there for decades and was part
of my own prayer and ritual during my chemo. I know her spirit helped during my illness, so it was important to me and to my husband and family that
we plant the new flowering tree whose roots will intermingle underground
with my mother's plant roots."

7

SPECIAL TRIBUTES

A wedding vow renewal ceremony is perfect for expressing love and gratitude to all of the people in your life who have supported you and, by virtue of sharing your life, contribute to your lasting union. Here, you'll find out the most popular tributes that you can include in your ceremony.

Tributes to Your Families

- Present them with single long-stemmed roses.
- Present the ladies with bouquets or nosegays, and boutonnieres for the men.
- Present the ladies with floral bracelets to wear throughout the ceremony.
- Present them with gifts of jewelry. For example, you might give your daughters the same kind of diamond pendant necklace your husband gives you as a symbol of your vow renewal.
- In the same manner, give the kids birthstone pendants or rings, while your ring holds a collection of the same stones in a mother's ring setting.
- Give your mother a birthstone ring containing her birthstone and those of all of her children.
- Give the ladies heart lockets or heart charm bracelets.
- Perform a reading dedicated to your children, parents, or families.
- Plant a tree seedling to symbolize the growth of your family, or point out to your guests the mighty tree in the yard that you all planted together twenty-five years ago.

- Unveil a garden stone that's been inscribed with all of your names on it.
- Have a plaque created, inscribed with all of your names, and install it on your garden bench with a mention that your family will always have a seat waiting for them at home.

Tributes to Your Wedding

As a tribute to your wedding, you might choose to copy some of the elements from that day into this one. What fun it would be to wear your original wedding gown again! If it's hopelessly out of style or just not in condition to be worn, there are plenty of other options that add a personal touch and an air of sentimentality to your day.

- Create an exact replica of your original wedding bouquet, with the same types of flowers and arrangement.
- Walk down the same aisle runner you used at your wedding (if you bought or made it yourself back then).
- Use the same ceremony readings.
- Use the same ceremony music.
- Hire the same musicians who played at your wedding.
- Use the exact same wedding vows you spoke back then, adding new material to the end of them (see chapter 6) as an update.
- Use the same wedding bands you used back then, only this time have them upgraded with a new setting, an extra ring jacket, or a new inscription underneath that may be a surprise to your spouse (see chapter 11).
- Use the same rosary or handfasting cord in a portion of your ceremony.
- Use the same crowns that were used in your original ceremony.
- Conduct the same food or wine rituals as in your wedding ceremony.
- Even if you're not in a house of worship, request the same "exchanging of peace" ritual by asking everyone to greet or hug the people around them.

- Have the same attendants as the first time around.
- Present an offering to the same icon statue if you're marrying in a house of worship. To you, it could be all the more meaningful to offer roses to the statue you once kneeled in front of as a young couple.
- Walk back down the aisle to the same music as was played at your wedding.

Explain It All to the Newcomers

Some of your guests might not have been around for your original wedding, so share the deep meanings and sentimentality of your renewal ceremony elements with explanations in your printed program. An example would be *"Sarah is wearing the same dress she wore at the wedding, and her mother's saint's pendant is pinned to her bouquet . . . just like the first time."* Or, *"The attendants—Jane-Marie, Elise, and Jessica—were Sarah's original bridesmaids."* It's a wonderful way to share all of the special tributes of your day with the newcomers and younger generations, who will be inspired by the traditions you've kept. Plus, those younger generations might just adopt your idea and turn it into a *family* tradition to last for years and years to come.

Tributes to Each Other

Of course, you'll include tributes to each other in the form of the words you speak—the praise, the heartfelt memories shared, your new and improved vows—but you might choose an additional tribute or two for one another. These could be surprise gifts, such as a diamond pendant, a single daisy like the one you brought her on your first date, an inside joke like a little wink or a tug of your ear. You've been together for a long time, so you have an unspoken language between you. It could just be the slight lift of an eyebrow or a slight little smile that conveys an enormous message.

Another fine option is to present a tribute to each other in private. Before or after your vow renewal ceremony begins, you could take a moment to say a few private words that are for your spouse's ears only, have a champagne toast with arms encircled, or just hug and whisper an "I love you" in each other's ears. A great deal of your marriage has been between just the two of you, so at least a small part of this vow renewal ceremony could be for just the two of you as well. Fill these private moments with tributes you'll both always remember.

JEANNE BACH AND ROB CLARK, MARRIED MARCH 5, 1989,
RENEWED MARCH 18, 2005

"We chose the month of our wedding anniversary rather than our actual
anniversary day, because it was going to be the night of a full moon. We
made arrangements for a sunset wedding vow renewal ceremony in St.
John's and actually traded in our Virginia timeshare so that we could be in
the Virgin Islands and be someplace warm. We love the water and since we
met while on the water working as part of a charter crew for cruises, this
was the perfect chance for us to create the celebration that's most us. When
we originally married, it was on our lunch hour at a Ft. Lauderdale chapel.
So this time, we really wanted the ocean experience. We customized our
ceremony, asking our coordinator to get a Tahitian hei for each of us. A hei
is just like a Hawaiian lei, except it's worn as a crown on the head. Plus, we
were able to read the vows we'd originally written for our wedding, which
was very important to us since we almost didn't have our original ceremony
when our officiant at the time wouldn't let us customize our vows to our
liking. We did so now, and we loved our officiant's closing wording:
'Acknowledge the past and let it go. All problems from the past, let them
go. This is a true renewal for the marriage.' With the sunset over the ocean
as our ceremony's final scene, it was just perfect . . . sixteen years later."

8

CLOSING MOMENTS

In the wedding scene from the movie *Love, Actually*, the bride and groom's walk back down the aisle is interrupted by a surprise musical performance arranged by the best man (okay, so the best man was secretly in love with the bride, but let's hope that won't be the case at your renewal celebration). The opening notes from the song "All You Need Is Love" begin playing, a choir sings in the balcony, a vocalist steps out from behind a curtain, and various musical artists (trumpeters, flutists, etc.) stand up among the wedding guests—all to serenade the couple. The exit, then, is a festive and sentimental one, a surprise to your guests, and perhaps even a surprise to your partner if you make the arrangements.

For years, the walk back down the aisle after a wedding ceremony concludes—and now, after a wedding vow renewal ceremony concludes—has had its traditions. The guests applaud, a trumpet voluntary is sounded, or the strains of Vivaldi's *Four Seasons* signal the start of the recessional. Perhaps the bride and groom jump the broom to signal the start of their new life together. But now, for *you*, this previously traditional moment in time can be something entirely new. Something very *you*.

If it seems we're taking all of the first-time wedding traditions and giving them a personalized twist, you're absolutely right. You're not constrained by any proper wedding protocol! You could strap on a pair of Rollerblades and skate back down the aisle together if you'd like—you wouldn't be the first couple to exit on that note. Feel like jumping on a motorcycle to speed away from your outdoor renewal ceremony? Again, you wouldn't be breaking new ground on that one.

Here are some ways to exit your vow renewal ceremony in style, and perhaps even with laughter, broken down into indoor versus outdoor options. The indoor ideas are those things you could do while walking back down the aisle together, hand in hand, after you seal your renewed vows with a kiss. The outdoor ones are, obviously, those fabulous "driving off into the sunset" moments that conclude your ceremony . . . even if you just drive around the block and then return for your reception. You'll still get those great going-away pictures.

Indoor Closing Moments

- Copy the movie *Love, Actually*. Arrange for a musical serenade by a vocalist, a choir, a jazz saxophonist, harpists, an a capella group, a Frank Sinatra impersonator, even a trio of drummers or bagpipers. You can find unique musicians (one couple found Native American drummers, while another found an Italian opera soprano) through musical associations, colleges or performing arts schools, and special event entertainment companies online. Again, you could plan this musical send-off as a surprise to your mate, a little gift before the party starts. (See chapter 15 for more information on entertainment.)

- Play a festive song. In the absence of Native American drummers or opera sopranos, you could simply turn up the CD player with a festive song that says "Let's get ready to celebrate!" When the song begins, you'll get your guests up on their feet, clapping along, and the fun begins. Some idea for songs to consider: "Let's Get It Started" by the Black-Eyed Peas (which several couples have told me their *grandchildren* picked out for them), "My Girl" by the Temptations, "Conga" by Miami Sound Machine, "All Night Long" by Lionel Ritchie, and, in the slower category "What a Wonderful World" by Louis Armstrong. For more closing moment song ideas, check out the suggestions on www.weddingchannel.com.

- Still keeping with the musical theme, you could play a love song and dance together back down the aisle.

- Your renewal ceremony could conclude with a song or a musical performance by someone whose act is their gift to you . . . and a lovely and unforgettable sentimental layer to your special moment. It will mean all the more to honor your child's singing talents (and perhaps her aspirations for a musical career) by letting her sing as your ceremony's closing act. Your father could play his guitar, together with your son, as a meaningful moment for you all to absorb. After all, it's always been family tradition for the two of them to play in front of the fireplace at Thanksgiving. Bringing that moment to *your* moment now . . . that's priceless.
- Be serenaded by all of your guests. Make a note in your ceremony programs that after your renewal kiss, everyone is invited to sing you off on your way with a group rendition of—hey, why not!— "All You Need Is Love." Again, check lyrics sites to get the wording for your programs.
- Take each other's hand for your exit and then stop and take your children's hands as well . . . you'll all exit together, as a family.
- Toss your bouquet. Why wait for the reception, as traditional first-time brides do. You can toss your bouquet into the guests' seating area as a way to immediately send off a positive superstition and symbol to the next to marry. If you don't want to part with your bouquet just yet, you can pick up a nosegay waiting on a chair nearby and throw that one to your guests. Or choose a bouquet that's called a breakaway, a ribbon-tied bouquet that—when the main ribbon is removed—breaks down into six to eight mini ribbon-tied clusters of flowers. When you throw the bunch, they separate in the air, and a half dozen or so lucky recipients catch them.
- Hand out flowers. As you depart, you'll take a moment to hand out single long-stemmed roses to your kids, your mothers, your grandmothers, your godmothers, and the woman who originally introduced you all those years ago. Roses can be given to couples or to men as well.

Outdoor Closing Moments

- If your ceremony will be held outdoors, the sky is the limit. So send something off into the sky, such as a butterfly release or a flight of doves (see Resources). I'd suggest that you skip the colorful release of helium balloons, as those latex or Mylar balloons can eventually come back down to earth in the form of a danger to animals or the environment.

- Twist the traditional. While wedding couples jump into a limousine or car with a Just Married sign on the back, *you* get to jump into a decorated car or convertible (or limo, if you wish!) with a unique take on the Just Married sign. Some ideas: *Just Re-Married, STILL Married, Happily Married*, or *And They Said It Wouldn't Last!* Or create a sign surrounded by flowers with your names and the number of years you've been married.

- If you're riding off in a limo, open the sunroof and stand up to wave to your guests.

- If you're on the beach, take a romantic walk into the sunset.

- In a true fairy-tale scene, a waiting horse and carriage can take you to your reception. You can choose from a number of styles and sizes, such as a glass-enclosed carriage or an open-air carriage decorated beautifully with flowers, garlands, and that modern-twist sign. Check the site for Carriage Operators of North America (www.cona.org) to find certified horse and carriage operations near you.

- If you're in a winter wonderland for your ceremony, book a horse and sleigh with a driver dressed in Victorian garb.

- Book a luxury or classic car. When you first married, there might not have been stretch Lincoln Navigators on the market. Or perhaps you didn't have the budget for a Rolls-Royce or Bentley. Now, you can choose from among thousands of luxury or classic cars, whether antique or a shiny new stretch version. We'll say more on fabulous wheels in chapter 19.

- Sail off into the sunset . . . or the night sky. Couples who renew their vows at a marina club or other spot right on the water can

step onto the deck of a yacht or schooner that's been decorated
with strings of white lights. As your boat sails away, you can pop
the cork of a champagne bottle and enjoy your first toast together
on the smooth seas as your guests wave from dockside. Need to
find a charter company? Check online or at the tourism department (www.towd.com) for referrals.

- And of course, there's always a waiting motorcycle, which could
even be your renewal gift to your husband . . . or his to you.

Part 3
WHAT TO WEAR

CAROL AND JEFF COHEN, MARRIED NOVEMBER 9, 2002, RENEWED NOVEMBER 18, 2004, ON *GOOD MORNING AMERICA* AT THE HAMMERSTEIN BALLROOM IN NEW YORK CITY

"Right before our engagement, we found ourselves under the Twin Towers in the World Trade Center shopping mall complex on September 11. The planes hit as we ran out of the buildings to safety. Unfortunately, eleven of our colleagues were not so lucky that day and met their fate in the Towers. We decided to get married on November 9, reversing the numbers, in honor of the tragic event.

"Beyond that experience, our first year of marriage saw tremendous health challenges with our family. Jeff's mom was diagnosed with breast cancer. Jeff's sister was bedridden for six months as she struggled through a twin pregnancy. Jeff's beloved Grandma was diagnosed with Alzheimer's and began losing her short-term memory. Jeff's elderly aunt broke her hip and needed Jeff to take over her bill paying and medical care. Meanwhile, my father spent a month in the hospital with diabetes-related complications. Needless to say, these health issues made it extremely difficult to spend quality time as a newlywed couple and settle into our first year of marriage. Renewing our vows was the perfect way to get a fresh start after battling the health issues."

Jeff and Carol Cohen were chosen by Good Morning America to be among a group of specially selected couples who would renew their vows in a beautiful formal ceremony and celebration at the Hammerstein Ballroom in New York City. They received the celebrity treatment as a deserving couple in grand New York City style, and Carol was chosen from all of the included couples to model her new Watters and Watters cream-colored gown in a fashion show on television. Following the group vow renewal ceremony, all of the couples were given the surprise gift of a honeymoon cruise.

9

YOUR DRESS

Choosing your dress for the big day can be every bit as magical as when you first shopped for your wedding gown. Perhaps even moreso if you're thrilled at not being limited to a proper dress in virginal white, a modest cut, or obscenely high designer wedding gown prices for a dress that tradition dictates is only worn once. This time, any color is open to you; you can go sophisticated and sleek, sexy and strapless, or leg-baring if you'd like; glamorous, or chic, simple, and streamlined. Your dress is an expression of who you are now and what your renewal celebration dream entails.

Your gown or dress is part of your story, so it might find you, rather than the other way around.

Whatever your style, the most important aspect of your dress is that you feel terrific in it, that it just feels right to you, and that you shine in it. Whether you're in a designer gown or a bright red cocktail dress, the dress will be perfect for you.

Formality Chart

Of course, the gown or dress you choose must fit with the formality of your planned event. A ball gown or floor-length gown is ideal for your formal ceremony and celebration, while a strapless sundress works for your relaxed and casual garden ceremony. Here are the basics on formality rules, which do govern the choices you make but still allow you plenty of freedom to select the style that's most you.

Ultraformal (white tie and black tie evening celebrations)
- Full-length ball gown
- Elbow-length gloves as ideal accents to reflect formality

Formal
- Full-length gown
- Bi-level gown: long in the back, calf-length in the front
- Cocktail-length gown, well accessorized for a more formal look

Semiformal
- Cocktail-length gown
- Knee-length gown
- Dressy pantsuit, well accessorized to dress it up

Informal
- Knee-length dress
- Pantsuit

Casual
- Knee-length dress
- Sundress

Ultracasual
- Khaki long skirt and colored or white top
- Jeans and floral or solid-color top
- Bathing suit and sarong

You've dressed for formal and informal weddings before, so the same rules apply. Just follow basic fashion common sense, tie your formality into your style and the time of day, and of course if you'll hold your ceremony in a house of worship, ask about their rules on no bare shoulders and other restrictions that could affect your dress choices.

That Color Looks *Great* On You

Yes, you *can* wear white if you wish. After all, today's first-time brides are wearing colored gowns, so why pass up that beautiful white dress because of an outdated rule? You can wear any color you wish, even black for a stylish and sophisticated look if that's your dream. Today's dresses are available in an array of vivid and bright colors, elegantly pearl-colored and shimmering with a satin shine or textured and brocaded, that you have the entirety of the fashion world at your disposal. There's never been a better time to dress up for a party, and since this is your big party, make your dress memorable. It's your chance to make your husband's jaw drop open again, just like it did on your wedding day when he first saw you in your wedding gown.

The most popular color choices for renewal ceremonies are:

- *Lights*—Champagne-colored or ivory, blush pink, lavender, coral, light blue
- *Brights*—Red, salmon, teal
- *Darks*—Black, cranberry, burgundy, hunter green, navy

Style Points

You know the style of dress that looks great on you, the type of neckline, the taper of the waist, the length that makes you look taller, the cut that makes you look thinner. You know the amount of décolletage that you're comfortable with, the amount of skin you're comfortable showing. You also know your body. You know that you'd like to show off those biceps you've been working so hard to shape or that you'd be more comfortable hiding your upper arms from view with a great sleeve that makes you *look* more toned.

While you know your body and your own sense of style, I do encourage you to explore different choices a little bit. Take advantage of your dress shopping excursion to experiment with a different kind of style. Perhaps a halter top or a strapless top, a more fitted skirt—something you wouldn't ordinarily wear. Just think about all of those makeover shows on television. The fashion experts only have to do a little bit of nudging to get a clothing-shy woman to step into a sheath or a fitted jacket, a sexier style, and then the subject is twirling in front of a mirror in pure bliss, never having known she could look so good. All it took was a little bit of courage to try a new style. That could be you twirling in front of the mirror. You might redefine your own sense of style, opening up a new fashion world for yourself. You might discover that you are indeed a halter kind of woman or that this is a new era for you. You're going to dress with more style, rather than stick with your old, safe comfort clothes.

Check out the many dress styles on bridal Web sites. Look at not just wedding gowns but bridesmaids' gowns and dresses as well. That's where the wealth of designer styles are. That's where fashion gets fun. Check out the new options in two-piece dresses, mixing and matching your choice of top (strapless, halter, princess neckline) with your choice of skirt (A-line, ball gown, slit sheath). Look at dresses that have *illusion netting* sewn in, a transparent or lacy patch of fabric that covers you, but lets some skin show through, such as on your arms, your neckline, or even your stomach if you have a toned tummy to show off. It all depends on your comfort level and also what's age-appropriate for you. Keep in mind that the term "age-appropriate" has changed: fifty-year-old women can pull off a sexy sheath dress way better than some twenty-year-olds. So where do you place yourself on the age-appropriate scale? For you, a classic silk pantsuit may be perfection or a floral sundress may be just what you had in mind. What style fits you best?

Need some extra help? You could go to a department store and sign up for a personal shopping service. It's free, and the style designers will interview you for your preferences, take your measurements, then pull a selection of dresses and accessories that will be waiting for you in the dressing room. It's the VIP treatment, with expert fashion advice. You could learn more about which dress styles suit you and your occasion, and perhaps pick up the perfect shoes and accessories to match.

Mary Jo Matsumoto, style columnist at SheKnows.com has the following style tips for you.

Your Personal Red Carpet—Women who want their wedding vow renewal to be a glamorous affair can opt for shimmer and sparkles most commonly seen on evening wear. If sequins and beaded lace don't suit you, plunging necklines or bare shoulders add a touch of confident style.

Princess for a Day—To look like a goddess for your wedding vow renewal ceremony choose a beautiful draped Grecian-influenced style. A better choice for tall and statuesque women, this type of gown conjures a romantic, sexy, and glamorous feeling all at once.

Fashionable Alternative to White—A gold dress is regal and perfect for women who want to wear something more conservative or traditional but who also want an elegant change from eggshell or cream. Available in head-to-toe honey-toned gowns, you can also choose from metallic embroidery detailing or gold fleur-de-lis–influenced prints.

Tailored Classic—Tailoring and luxury are always stylish and classic at the same time. One particularly nice choice for a wedding vow renewal ceremony is a classic shirtwaist-style floor-length dress. The silhouette becomes even more opulent in glossy satin.

The Dress You Never Had—If you dreamed of a haute-couture creation for your first wedding but spending a year's salary for a couture dress is not an option, you can still wear something fabulous. Have a custom-made gown designed that is similar to your favorite runway creation and live your fantasy!

In the Garden—Renewing wedding vows in the garden has a simple and nostalgic feel. Your outfit should reflect this tone. It's appropriate to wear anything from a full-length white wedding gown to a more casual short dress. A fitted suit or, alternatively, a dress with a matching morning coat in cream or soft garden colors is another flattering choice. Choose fabrics such as cottons, linen, silks, or chiffons, which have a sweet outdoors feel in keeping with your location.

At the Beach—A more carefree setting such as a local or even faraway destination beach ceremony means attire will most likely reflect a more flowing, easygoing feel. A fitted sheath may be your choice for a simple, elegant style, or you may wish for a fitted top and breezy skirt.

Off-the-shoulder short dresses worn with a flower tucked behind one ear are often worn at beach ceremonies, and anything goes in terms of footwear—flowered flip-flops and bare feet fit right in. If the ceremony is planned in the patio or garden of a formal hotel with a beach back-drop, a more formal satin gown and heels can also be appropriate. Stick to solids and avoid sequined or embellished looks.

What Your Attendants Will Wear

It's usually not necessary to require your daughters, friends, or other at-tendants to select and order matching bridesmaid-type dresses, unless of course your vow renewal celebration will be a formal or ultraformal wedding do-over where it just seems ideal to have all of your atten-dants in matching styles. You could, as a gracious host, tell your chosen attendants that it's their choice. They can either choose matching bridesmaid-style gowns in the same manner as for a wedding, or you can all head to a department store to shop the formal dress racks to-gether. Keep in mind that in January, holiday formal gowns and party dresses are on sale, and the prom dresses are starting to come in. To-day's prom gowns and dresses are highly fashionable, sophisticated, and some are outright sexy. You'll find plenty of options to choose from, in a range of colors, and in a range of sizes if you shop early enough.

Since it's not a must to have everyone in a matching dress, open the options to allow your attendants to choose dresses in their own style choices. Some might want strapless, some might want halter, and others might want a full-coverage top. Since an A-line skirt is the type that flatters the most body types, that's a good option to make all of your attendants comfortable. Keep in mind that your attendants could range in age as your daughters, granddaughters, friends, and even your mother and grandmother are all eligible for spots in your attendant lineup. Finding one style to suit them all might be close to impossible, so a group shopping trip with your eye on one color could be a great day at the mall for all of you. Just bring the dresses close together to check the color comparison. Your version of pink could be very different from another person's. Or, their colors can coordinate, with a range of pinks and reds according to their choices, skin tones, and preferences ("I look awful in light pink! Can I go more coral?").

In situations where everyone lives in a different state, you could send them a link to a dress you found online or ask them to choose their style in your chosen color from your favorite dress Web site. Or, give them the freedom to choose their own dress, or perhaps wear one they own, with your simple directive of "Wear a black cocktail dress."

When your ceremony and celebration are less formal, you can ask your attendants to wear whatever they'd like, whether they match or not. For you, it's more important that they're *there*, not what they're wearing.

For your little girls in the "bridal party," they can wear their own party dresses rather than buy new ones, or coordinate their own little white party dresses with new sashes you've chosen, and perhaps made, in the color of your choice. Again, the little girls don't have to match identically. If they already own matching party dresses, wonderful. If not, then it's either a shopping trip or a quick accessory add-on (like a sash) or matching floral nosegays—with the colors of each of their dresses—to tie their coordinating looks together.

Accessories

Dressing up your dress can make your look extra-special. From shoes to a silk scarf to the sapphire earrings and necklace set your husband gave you for your birthday, your style choices are completely up to you. Will you wear something new, something old, something blue (like those sapphires)?

Shoes—Select a great shoe, both for its beauty and for its comfort. Remember, you'll likely be on your feet for hours that day, dancing, mingling, going back up to that chocolate fountain for the tenth time.

A wider, thicker heel could give you better ankle support and makes walking easier if you'll be on grass as it will keep you from sinking into soft ground. If you'll be on the beach, you might be barefoot or wearing a pair of cute beach sandals with a floral accent at the toe.

Jacket or Wrap—If all or part of your event will take place out-doors—in a garden or yard, on the beach, on a boat—you'll need a great jacket or wrap to coordinate with your dress. Look at fabulous shawls or even a beautifully crocheted jacket that you can wear for a higher formality in your ceremony, then remove to reveal a sleek halter dress underneath for the celebration.

Hat—Check department stores for their range of styles, or check out a milliner (find one online) for a custom design to perfectly compliment your dress.

Gloves—Your formality level might call for elbow-length gloves, as in the case of an ultraformal event. Or, as a matter of style, you might wish to wear shorter or wrist-length gloves, lace or crocheted gloves. You can find a range of gloves in various colors and styles either online, through bridal Web sites, at bridal dress shops, or in the accessory section of your favorite department store.

Undergarments—Wearing the right bra can make your dress look even better. Stepping into a bodyslimmer—which is all the rage right now, even among trim celebrities—can take literal inches off your silhouette, and great stockings compliment your legs.

Jewelry—We'll talk about rings and jewelry in a later chapter. Right now, think about any special jewelry sets your husband has given you—or that you've bought for yourself—as a possibility for your big day.

JANINE GORDON AND ALVIN SCHECHTER, MARRIED OCTOBER 13, 2004,
RENEWED MARCH 11, 2005

*"For our wedding ceremony, we actually 'eloped' to City Hall on October
13, 2004, for a civil ceremony. Five months later, we resanctified our vows
in front of all our friends and family. Given the venue of the celebration,
the engraved invitation read: From City Hall . . . to CITY HALL (a
famed restaurant in New York City). The groom wore black tie. The bride
wore a one-hundred-year-old cream-colored silk kimono (which had been
deaccessioned from a private collection) heavily embroidered with pale, pale
wisteria. The groom is, in fact, a retired world-class designer whose company was responsible for logos, brand development, and design systems for
companies ranging from Coca-Cola to Taco Bell to R.J. Reynolds. He now
designs furniture and renovates old houses, so he had a particular interest in
the details of our event. Incidentally, the groom is seventy-one and the bride
fifty-something. Love springs eternal."*

10

THE "GROOM" AND HIS MEN

Your husband looks so handsome in a tuxedo, doesn't he?

Whether he'll wear a tuxedo or his favorite, most dashing suit with the tie you gave him for his birthday, your husband and the men of his lineup (including sons and perhaps grandsons) will dress for the occasion. Granted, you may be of the casual variety and your dress code means khaki pants and a white shirt for the men, and they already have those in their closets. Your selection of men's wardrobe will have everything to do with the formality and style of the renewal celebration you have in mind. Your men will need to match the scene, and they'll look quite suave in all those photos as well.

Here are the wardrobe guidelines for each level of formality, and rules apply to all men in the "bridal party." Fathers and grandfathers may also join in the dress code if they wish, especially for those ultra-formal wedding do-overs where the men finally get to wear that Ralph Lauren tuxedo style you both wanted all those years ago.

Ultraformal Evening (commonly called "white-tie")
- Black tailcoat tuxedo, also known as "black full dress" or white tailcoat with wing-collared white shirt
- White vest or black vest
- White bow tie (tie and vest are in matching color, whether black or white)

Ultraformal Daytime
- Black or gray waistcoat or gray cutaway coat or gray cutaway tuxedo

* Pants: gray tuxedo or gray pinstriped
* White wing-collar of fold-collar shirt
* Gray vest
* Gray solid, striped, or four-in-hand tie or ascot

Formal Evening (commonly called "black-tie")

* Black tuxedo jacket or black tailcoat or black stroller coat
* In spring or summer, white or pastel tuxedo or cutaway jackets are okay with matching or black tuxedo pants
* White wing-collar shirt
* Black bow tie or black long tie
* Black cummerbund or vest

Formal Daytime

* Gray cutaway tuxedo or gray tuxedo jacket (worn with gray pin-striped pants)
* Black or gray morning coat or gray waistcoat (paired with black-and-gray pinstriped pants)
* Light-colored, cream, or white jacket
* White spread-collar shirt or white wing-tipped shirt
* Ties or vests in color or coordinating print

Semiformal Evening

* Black tuxedo or black suit
* White dinner jacket with formal black pants
* White or colored wing-tipped collar, turned-down collar, or mandarin collar shirt
* Black or color-coordinated long tie
* Color-coordinated vest or cummerbund

Semiformal Daytime

* Gray stroller coat, navy suit jacket, gray suit jacket, or black suit jacket
* White or tan linen suits in summer

- Pants to match suit jackets
- White, colored, or striped dress shirt
- Color-coordinated four-in-hand (or full-length) tie
- Gray vest
- No cummerbunds for this style

Informal Daytime

- Navy, gray, or tan suit
- Navy blazer and white shirt with khaki pants (the classic look most popular for this style of event)
- White or colored button-down shirt with khaki pants, with or without long tie
- Solid or patterned, color-coordinating tie (optional) or a theme-print tie for fun

Informal Evening

- Dark suits with white shirts, coordinating ties appreciated but optional
- Dinner jacket worn with khaki or suit pants, paired with white or colored button-down shirt, tie appreciated but optional

Ultracasual

- Khaki shorts with white or hued button-down shirts
- Jeans with white or hued button-down shirts
- Bathing suit on the beach

Matching Up Your Men

At your wedding, you may have gone traditional, with all the men from your groom to the groomsmen to the ring bearer, fathers, and grandfathers in matching tuxedoes. Only your groom had a white bow tie to set him apart. The look was dashing and debonair. The men never looked better.

Now, for your renewal ceremony, you may choose to do the same if your event will be a formal wedding do-over. (In this instance, you may finally have the resources to get those matching tuxes for all!) This may even be your husband's great wish, as so many men request this matching-look for all of the men right down to the same burgundy vests and silver cuff links for the men of the bridal party, with that white vest and tie for your husband. It looks great in person and in the pictures.

Decide which of your men will adhere to the dress code formality rules. Will your sons and fathers also rent tuxedoes? If your husband will have a best man, he too ought to be dressed in a similar style as the "groom," which may mean a tuxedo rental for him as well. The men should match in the case of a formal renewal event.

When the event is less formal, such as a ceremony where the husband will wear his own suit, the most common arrangement is for any men of the "bridal party" including teenage sons and young sons, fathers and grandfathers, to wear similarly colored suits of their own. There's no need to take everyone on a shopping trip to buy matching suits. What they own is fine, provided it fits well. "We decided that just I, our sons, and our fathers would wear suit jackets, and we instructed all of our guests to dress casually for our outdoor renewal event," says Dr. Chris Kammer, whose story is on page 128. "We wanted everyone in attendance to be relaxed and not feel like they had to dress formally, and we still had our own dress-up moment among our closest family members for the ceremony."

Some renewal couples welcome the idea of dressing more casually, out of a sense of comfort and planning for great family portraits where all of the men and kids look crisp and happy in their khaki pants and blue button-down shirts. Even the little guys. To set the "groom," sons, fathers, and any male attendants apart, this khaki-casual look can be accented with navy blazers (a great summer look) or matching ties. Some playful couples even give their main men pairs of stylish sunglasses to wear during the processional and recessional. Some other often-mentioned ideas: at ultracasual celebrations, the men wear matching T-shirts in a solid color or with a saying on them (like the

"Life Is Good" logo T-shirts), or a playful T-shirt with a tuxedo jacket graphic on it (see page 120 for Cher Floyd's renewal event . . . the groom wears one of these T-shirts). The men can wear crisp white shirts with their khakis and then coordinate by wearing matching yellow LIVEStrong wristbands or the shell necklaces that are all the rage for men on the islands.

Finding Formal Wear

Leaning toward the tuxedo style, but it's been a while since the wedding? The newest styles and designer names in tuxedo-land can be quite confusing, so ask a recently married couple for referrals on tuxedo shops and perhaps the name of a helpful stylist. To find a reputable rental agency near you, check with the International Formalwear Association (see Resources). As a smart consumer, you know that membership in any society or organization is a good sign that a shop is well-rated, established for a certain number of years, and owners and staff are sure to be trained and knowledgeable in the latest and greatest information in tuxedo design and styles. Membership is *not* an automatic yes, though. Be sure that you tour and interview well to find the shop that has the goods *and* a great guide.

You may also wish to invest in a tuxedo. Go to high-end discount stores like Nordstrom Rack and Off Fifth (Saks Fifth Avenue's outlet) to check out terrific buys on a budget. After one or two wearings, the tuxedo pays for itself in saved rental fees, and you have the perfect tuxedo to justify planning formal dates with each other as well!

Sprucing Up His Tried-and-True Suit and Tie

Since most men would rather wear a suit of their own to the renewal, trendy as they may be with their current collection of office and evening suits, there's still an option to "dress up" their big day wardrobe with the simple addition of a new shirt or new tie. Here are some of the styles to consider, and your man might just find a new favorite look.

THE HOTTEST NEW TREND FOR MEN: PERSONAL STYLISTS

They're also called personal shoppers, and a wide range of department stores and clothing boutiques offer the services of an on-staff fashion genius who will size up your man and ask a few questions about his personal sense of style and the style of your special event. You'll then make an appointment with the stylist, and when you show up, he or she will have already collected a range of suits, shirts, ties, shoes, accessories, and other fabulous finds for a streamlined try-on session with items chosen personally for your man. The guys love the customized collection waiting for them in the dressing room (just don't call it the *Pretty Woman* treatment, although that's exactly what it is), and they get to skip the dreaded picking through the racks part of the mall excursion. Personal shoppers and stylists are available at such stores as Nordstrom, Lord and Taylor, Bloomingdales, and others, plus at smaller boutiques you can find in a quick online search. Stylists work on commission, and some will even come to your *home* (sometimes for a small fee) to take a look through his closet for an expert-trained eye on how to update and accessorize the perfect outfit for the big day—and perhaps inspire him to upgrade the rest of his wardrobe, jackets, shoes, and work suits as well.

He may consider a new style of shirt, such as a wing-collar formal, crossed-collar formal, mandarin band collar, crossover collar, french cuffs, new designer collections in stripes and patterned stitching, or ethnic patterns.

If he'd like a new vest, consider 5-8-button styles, fullback (in which the back is entirely covered by fabric), open-backed (that cover the front, leave the back open, and attach around the waist), 100 percent silk, shiny or patterned fabrics in color-coordinates, ethnic and cultural choices, lighter colors for springtime and summertime events, geometric patterns, or fun party theme designs like wine bottles or sailboats.

Could his tie collection use a restyling? Now's the perfect opportunity to upgrade his assortment (and finally get rid of that superwide orange tie!). Consider classic bow ties in 100 percent silk or silk blends, 100 percent silk or silk blend long ties, long ties in a colored sheen or pattern, or a tie to match the color of his eyes (*sigh* . . .).

Shoes and Accessories

Another new purchase might be new shoes and accessories, although his already-owned dress shoes with a fresh shine might be perfectly fine for your event. If he does wish to spring for the new shoes, that's terrific. Or, you might be happy if all he does is spruce up the ones he has. As far as accessories, he might use the cuff links he wore at your wedding, the tie he wore at your wedding (provided it's still in great shape and in fashion), or the tie clip from the night of your engagement. Consider cuff link and studs ideas for a potential shopping trip and surprise from you to him: gold, white-gold or silver, engraved, black onyx, diamond-accent, laser-cut monogram, or antique-cut.

DR. CHRIS KAMMER AND JEAN MARIE KAMMER, MARRIED JUNE 15, 1985,
RENEWED JUNE 15, 2005

Dr. Chris Kammer planned a sparkling surprise for his wife Jean Marie on the occasion of their twentieth anniversary vow renewal celebration (see page 128 for more on their reception style). He says, "I had her wedding ring upgraded to a new platinum setting, and I also surprised her with a new anniversary band with twenty diamonds around the circle to wear with it."

11

RINGS AND OTHER JEWELRY FOR
YOUR RENEWAL CEREMONY

There's no time like now to start jewelry shopping! One of the top trends in wedding vow renewals is the giving of jewelry to one another . . . and to your kids as a meaningful memento of your celebration. Here, you'll start thinking about what your own jewelry options are.

Upgrading Your Wedding Rings

It doesn't take away an ounce of the symbolism if you change your wedding ring now. Although some renewal couples say they wouldn't dream of altering the rings they exchanged on their wedding day, others lean more toward "It's an enhanced version of the original." Perhaps you bought your original wedding rings when you were young. You loved a more ornate style but could better afford a simpler style. If you've always dreamed of adding diamonds to your wedding band or choosing a lower or more modern setting for your stone, now is the time.

This trend doesn't just apply to the wives. Husbands too are meaningfully embedding a diamond chip into their smooth platinum wedding bands or switching their somewhat too ornate 1980s band with swirly detailing for a more modern, sleek, unadorned platinum ring. He's changed a lot in the past decades, so his taste in wedding rings may have as well.

Diamond baguettes may be added to either side of your engagement ring, since that ring too is on your hand daily and thus an ideal spot for an additional sparkle. Think of your engagement ring and wedding band as one unit, since they're always together. Both are eligible for upgrading. And then of course, there's the new anniversary band studded with diamonds or gemstones, such as the one shown in Jean Marie Kammer's photo at the start of this chapter.

DON'T TOUCH MY RING!

If you'd rather not alter your original wedding ring in any way—you want it exactly the way it looked on your wedding day—you can upgrade in the form of a ring jacket. You'll slip your original wedding band or engagement ring into the space between two attached circular bands featuring either diamonds or gemstones. The result is your original ring surrounded by what looks like two new rings. Many couples say the triple look calls to that "past, present, and future" effect that's so hot in jewelry right now. Ask your jeweler to show you the latest styles in elegant or trendy ring jackets as a way to accessorize your wedding rings.

Getting a New Ring

It's not pure vanity that's sending couples to the jewelry store for brand new wedding rings to mark this sentimental occasion. While there certainly are couples who take the whole do-over practice to the extreme, replacing their simple wedding bands with extravagant new models, sometimes the reason is more practical.

- "I had lost my engagement ring while on vacation many years ago and was heartbroken. Replacing it with a new one then was out of the question, but now that we're renewing our vows, this is the perfect opportunity. It's always made me sad to be without it for so long, and now it feels right to replace it . . . since we have a new ceremony to go with it."
- "My husband developed arthritis over the years, and with his

swollen knuckles, he just can't get his wedding ring on. Now, we'll have the chance to get him a new one that he can wear, one with the diamond chips he always wanted."

- "I chose gold metal for my wedding ring back when I got married, and now I far prefer silver jewelry. My tastes have changed, so I'll take the stones from my ring and choose the exact same design, only in a platinum setting. That will allow me to get the kind of silver jewelry I love and match my style, which is much better than disliking my gold band ring for what it prevents me from wearing."

Of course, it doesn't always have to be a matter of a rough ocean wave knocking your ring away from you or arthritic fingers that might have you considering brand new rings. And it doesn't always have to be your hunger for a much bigger stone, embarrassed as you are that all the interns at your office have much more elaborate engagement rings than yours. Sometimes, it's just a wish:

- "I always said I wanted to get a ring that has my husband's and my birthstone set together. This is the perfect time to do that."
- "It means the world to us that I would wear a ring with both of our birthstones, plus those of our children. At the renewal ceremony, my husband will give mine to me, and then we'll give individual birthstone rings to the kids as a surprise. Even better, we're renewing our vows on Mother's Day."

Ring Engravings

Even if you had your wedding bands engraved for your wedding, you can still commemorate your renewal ceremony with a new engraving. This is one of the most popular options for those who either don't wish to change or upgrade their rings or whose budgets don't allow for a new rock or new setting.

Of course, if you didn't have your rings engraved back then, it's a fine option for now! Talk with your ring specialist about the ideal word placement on the insides of your bands. You can set words any-place you wish, even on the sides of your bands with super-fine print if you have a thicker band. Let's say your existing ring engraving reads:

M—*I Love You*—A

You can now alter that to:

M—*I Love You*—A

I Still Do—6/1/06

Your choice of engraving wording can be anything you wish, from an expression of love, a nickname, the dates of your wedding and your renewal, or something more personal such as "You Make My Life Complete." Some couples use a phrase from a favorite song, perhaps their wedding song, or their wish for forever such as "Eternity." If the couple has gone through a rough time in the past, their engraving might read, "Unbreakable." One husband chose a personalized mes-sage: "You are the strongest woman on earth" after his wife beat leukemia and went into remission. A religious sentiment might be used, such as a line from a favorite Psalm or a simple "You are my great-est blessing."

Other popular options:

Now, Forever and Always (If you had "*Always*" on your original ring, this is a great way to upgrade it.)
Everlasting Love
Happily Ever After
You Bring Me Joy
Yours Forever

Aside From the Rings . . .

If you love your rings just the way they are, you can always present each other with different choices in renewal gifts. Talk to your jeweler about quality and style, and you can always custom-design your choices in-store or online (see Resources for sites with ring personalization templates that you can print out and bring to your jeweler for a one-of-a-kind gift from the heart).

Some ideas for non-ring gifts are:

Diamond earrings

Diamond tennis bracelet

Three-diamond "past, present, future" pendant

A set of necklace, bracelet, and earrings in your birthstone

Necklace, bracelet, or earrings in the birthstone of your wedding

This last option is one of the hottest new trends. You'll look at your wedding day as the birth of this wonderful relationship you're in, and thus give your marriage a birthday of its own. If you married in May, the birthstone of your wedding would be the emerald, for instance. That could be the gemstone used in this new renewal jewelry piece, and—as many couples report—a start to a new collection. As always, your sentimental jewelry pieces become heirlooms to pass down in your family.

BIRTHSTONE CHART

Whether it's for you, for your kids, or for the date of your wedding, here is the official chart of monthly birthstones.

January: Garnet

February: Amethyst

March: Aquamarine

April: Diamond

May: Emerald

June: Pearl

July: Ruby

August: Peridot

September: Sapphire

October: Opal

November: Citrine

December: Blue Topaz

See www.bluenile.com for examples of lovely birthstone pendant necklace and earring sets.

Three-stone Jewelry

You've seen the commercials for those three-stone pendants . . . a voice-over set against dramatic violin music says something to the effect of "For your past, present, and future" while diamonds catch the light and sparkle beyond belief. The three-stone symbolism caught on like wildfire, and now one of the top trends in wedding vow renewal gifts is the very same choice. It's deep and meaningful as a tribute to shared life, and some might say that three stones are better than one!

Check out the many three-stone options at your jewelry shop, choosing from pendants, earrings (clusters of three diamonds set in each), bracelets (three stones set in a silver bangle), even rings. If your jewelry shop isn't well-stocked, or if you have something more customized in mind, you can design and order your own three-stone jewelry online. See Resources for ideas.

Watches for Him . . . And Her

Perhaps your husband would rather have a fabulous watch than an engraving or upgrade to his wedding ring. That watch he wears every day is nice, but what about one with a sapphire-blue watchface, or shining and sleek silver lines, or the Rolex he's always wanted. Again, the men don't own this category, as women are reporting in that they'd love a great watch as well. After all, their sweethearts have already given them the three-stone pendant for their birthday, and they love the idea of his and hers timepieces.

You can have the backs engraved and honor the time you've spent together as a couple with a symbolic new gift to one another.

Gifts For the Kids

As mentioned earlier, this is a wonderful time to honor your children as well with the gift of a birthstone ring or diamond pendant, diamond tennis bracelet, pearl pendant or earrings. You can incorporate into your renewal ceremony a segment where you'll repeat vows to your children, and perhaps they'll make a vow to you, in a meaningful ritual that reaffirms your family bond as well as your own marriage vows. Sons are often given watches or tie clips with a diamond chip, cuff links, or rings of their own. You've then given them something to hand down to their own children someday.

CHER AND JOHN FLOYD, MARRIED APRIL 27, 1991,
RENEWED APRIL 17, 1996, AND MAY 14, 2005

"John and I have renewed our wedding vows twice now. On our five-year anniversary, April 27, 1996, we chartered a yacht and had the captain perform the ceremony on Highbourne Cay in the Exuma Islands. We invited all the local residents to the ceremony and some even put on a shirt. I wore a white bikini with a white chiffon cover-up and my maid of honor wore a yellow bikini. I was brought over by boat by the captain's son, where I joined the rest of the wedding party and guests. I used my original wedding veil and had the original florist ship similar flowers for us and the wedding party. We were remarried on the Island at sunset.

"This year, we had a trip planned for France and Italy and renewed our wedding vows on the Windstar Cruise lines with the captain renewing the vows at sunset off the Isle of Capri. I made my wedding wreath and flowers and wore a beautiful white tropical gown. Many of the new friends we met on the cruise attended the ceremony with champagne, chocolate-covered cherries, and tres leches wedding cake.

"I can't help myself—I am a true romantic. I have even hosted two weddings at our house on the water at sunset."

12

WEAR AND CARRY FLOWERS

Your bouquet . . . it brings back memories of the bridal bouquet you carried on your wedding day. Was your original everything you had hoped for? White roses, gardenias, stephanotis, the ultimate fantasy bouquet? Do you want another one just like that one, as a tribute to your wedding day and a symbol that you wouldn't change a thing? You can certainly arrange to copy your original design.

Or, you can go the opposite way, carrying a bouquet of brightly colored flowers, vivid oranges or reds that really stand out against your ivory or pale blue dress. Whatever you can imagine, be it traditional bridalesque blooms, brights, or wildflowers, your floral designer can create it for you.

While bouquet designs vary, the overall trend is for a smaller bouquet, not a draping cascade that can overpower you and virtually hide you from view. Naturals and brights are all the rage, as well as a distinct departure from those traditional bridal flowers mentioned earlier. Now the trend is in unique and textural blooms. I spoke with Casey Cooper, principal of Botanicals in Chicago (www.botanicalschicago.com), about what she's designing for today's bouquets. Here are some of her style points:

- "Even though you don't have to carry a bouquet for this ceremony, it's always a wonderful thing if you do. After all, the tradition of carrying fresh flowers goes back in history, deep with meaning and symbolism. It's a nice thing to hold on to, that fresh and lovely natural collection of flowers and greens."
- "What you're wearing will determine the design of bouquet you'll carry. It works with the lines and silhouettes of your dress, as the perfect accent at the front of your waist."

- "Your flower choices will play off the color of your dress as well. For a lavender dress, for instance, I would suggest a bouquet of periwinkle and hyacinths, tied with a deeper purple ribbon."
- "For a blue dress, you have access to the greatest trend in color combination—blues and greens or blues and chocolate browns. You have to see them together to appreciate the eye-catching combination of lady's mantle with the blue, or the chocolate fern curls with a chartreuse green floral mix, or chocolate cosmos with a sage green blend."
- "For a little black dress that's very tailored and sophisticated, imagine a little clutch of pink peonies or again gorgeous chartreuse green cymbidiums tied with a ribbon. Adding color to a black dress is always the way to go, as a cluster of white flowers wouldn't stand out as well."
- "Bouquets are getting more whimsical, more casual. Consider a bouquet of vibrant gerbera daisies in oranges and yellows for a spring or summer event. You'll always need to tie your flower choices in with the season, both for availability and pricing and also for more readily available other seasonal blooms to coordinate. Look outside of traditional bridal flowers."
- "And of course, going natural with unique flowers always makes a statement. I just designed a bouquet of Queen Anne's lace that was so natural and so lovely. It matched the bride's personality as well as her dress."

Symbolism works well with your bouquet choices. You could select the same type of flower your husband brings you for every special event, or your birth flower, or a family tribute flower such as the same gardenias you had in your bridal bouquet, your mother had in hers, your grandmother and great-grandmother, and so on. Or, add the symbolism into the construction of the bouquet itself, such as pinning a saint medallion onto your bouquet handle, just as you did at your wedding, or using a length of lace from your original gown for the handle of this bouquet. If you never preserved your gown and have no plans for it, it could be a very meaningful use of a salvageable section of your veil or leftover lace from one of your bridal projects back then. Bring a bit of then to now.

USING BIRTH MONTH FLOWERS

Just as you would select birthstone jewelry, you also have birth month flowers to consider as symbolic parts of your day. You could use a combination of your birth month flower and your husband's, the "birth month" of your marriage (the month of your wedding anniversary, that is), or a combination of your kids' birth month flowers together with yours in a family arrangement with meaning. Here are the traditional birth month flowers.

January: Carnation

February: Violet

March: Jonquil

April: Sweet pea

May: Lily of the valley

June: Rose

July: Larkspur

August: Gladiola

September: Aster

October: Marigold

November: Chrysanthemum

December: Narcissus

Additions to your bouquet now, which might not have been available when you married, might be pearl- or crystal-headed pushpins inserted into roses, strings of light-catching crystals woven through your bouquet or cascading delicately over the side. You might look at item push-ins such as a tiny silk butterfly in a tribute to your departed grandmother (butterflies were her favorite) or carry a bouquet of all greens or herbs rather than flowers (those darn allergies). A single red rose might be your choice, or a cluster of elegant hand-tied calla lilies in white, green, or a cabernet wine color.

In most cases, the trend is for the bouquet or hand-carried flowers to be your favorite blooms, something magical and sentimental from the tale of your shared history together. And to share that story with your guests in your printed program.

Flowers You'll Wear

Another top style choice, both for renewal ceremonies and for weddings, is incorporating floral touches in your hair or your jewelry: flowers you *wear*. The effect is a stunning, natural look and a new way to incorporate your favorite flower into your big day ensemble. Here are some of the hottest ideas, suggested by Casey Cooper of Botanicals:

Flowers in Your Hair
- Rather than affix a fresh flower, such as a gardenia, to a hairclip as an accent to your chignon, avoid all the extra weight and just have the gardenia pinned into your chignon
- Affix tiny delicate flowers into the loose ringlets of your hair
- Tuck a bright daisy or a hibiscus bloom behind your ear
- Wear a delicate floral wreath, embedded with both flowers and herbs
- Create a floral band effect by pinning small flowers in an arch across the top or bottom of an upsweep

Floral Jewelry
All manner of small flowers, from baby rosebuds to tiny diaises, hyacinths and lilies, can be turned into floral jewelry. Some examples for you, for your kids, your mothers, and even for the special women in your "bridal party."
- A ribbon bracelet with a single small flower attached
- A bracelet of tightly woven flowers, such as daisies or baby roses

- A thin or thick ribbon choker with a flower attached in the front
- A necklace with a flower as the pendant
- Hyacinth blossom earrings
- Lengths of ribbon tied with floral blooms or buds, crystals or pearls, woven into loosely flowing or upswept hair
- Floral pins or brooches

Some renewal couples give these out as welcome gifts to all of their female guests.

Talk with your floral designer about creating custom floral jewelry for you, or look at floral sites online for examples that you can show to your florist for your own design creation.

The Men's Boutonnieres

Your husband and his men should wear boutonnieres if they're wearing tuxedos, and boutonnieres can also be pinned onto their suit jackets for the day. As the man of the hour, your husband can select from a wide range of boutonniere blooms, again with the option of moving away from traditional bridal-type flowers such as roses and stephanotis if he wishes. The men can all wear matching boutonnieres, or follow the new style in assigning different flowers to different men. Casey Cooper suggests the following popular options for the guys' lapels.

- Dogwood blossoms
- Hypericum berry in the fall
- Goldenrod in the summer
- Succulents in tiny clusters
- An all-herb boutonniere, such as a rosemary cluster

The key, according to Casey, is to select flowers that are unique and eye-catching, full of great texture and color, but that also hold up well to their vertical position for lasting power through the day. No wilting allowed. Your wear-and-carry flowers should, of course, coordinate with the florals you've selected for your centerpieces and other decor. Those daisies then become a theme. Check out the floral centerpiece advice in Chapter 16 to help you make your decisions in this category as well.

Part 4

THE CELEBRATION

DR. CHRIS KAMMER AND JEAN MARIE KAMMER, MARRIED JUNE 15, 1985,
RENEWED JUNE 15, 2005

"All of my life, when I thought about marriage, I thought, Wouldn't it be great to be so happy and in love through the years that you'd remarry in a heartbeat? But suddenly, I found myself in the most recent two years of our marriage taking the good things for granted and focusing on the disappointments. I was operating on autopilot, just accepting how things were, and frankly having some tough times in the relationship. I felt like I was cheating my family, my wife, and myself by just going through the motions and accepting an 'okay' level of the commitment. So I sat down with my wife and my four kids—who came to us through the miracle of adoption and are all of different races—and made the announcement that a special day was coming up. I re-proposed to my wife in front of my children and took on the vow renewal plans as a gift to my wife and a way to get my family back on track. We held the celebration in our front yard, since I wanted our renewal to be out in the open. I didn't care about traffic or barking dogs. I wanted it to be publicly evident that this is where I'm coming from. I brought in our church choir to open the ceremony and to sing 'This Is Holy Ground.' Our friends provided the entertainment, the kids were in the bridal party, our neighbors made floral wreaths, and we had an informal barbecue as our reception. We celebrated our twenty years of marriage, and also honored our parents, who have a combined one-hundred-plus years of marriage between them. Everyone was moved to tears, and it was a beautiful celebration. I didn't want to go through life not having done this."

13

CHOOSING A RECEPTION STYLE

At the start of this book, you considered a range of celebration styles, from barefoot on the beach to a casual picnic in the backyard. Now, you're going to get more specific and really hone in on your chosen reception style. Choose from the following so that you can work with your caterer to plan your menu.

A Cocktail Party Only—Whether relaxed or semiformal, your guests will mingle and sample luscious choices from a buffet table or passed hors d'oeuvres. Seating would be unplanned, with couches or bistro tables set about the room for chatting and visiting.

A Cocktail Party with Buffet and Stations—The same as above, plus anywhere from three to six serving stations featuring sushi, seafood crepes, a pasta bar, seafood bar, soup bar, or other specialty spot where the chef does all the work.

A Traveling Cocktail Party—This trend started in the southern states and is taking over the world of celebrations. Guests begin in one room where a buffet is set up, and then everyone moves to another location (such as poolside) for an entirely different theme menu, such as cold seafood or fondues. Then, everyone will move to another location for different food selections, such as chafing dishes filled with hot choices or an ethnic menu featuring Thai food, and so on. With this "something new at every stop" arrangement, no one will miss a sit-down dinner. The last stop, of course, is desserts.

Cocktail Party and Sit-Down Dinner—Just like at a traditional wedding, the cocktail hour comes first, followed by a full five-course dinner and desserts.

Sit-Down Dinner, Served—Without the cocktail party, everyone takes their seats at long tables or place-arranged round tables and is served their five courses by waitstaff. Dessert, coffee, and after-dinner drinks might be served at another location or at the tables.

Sit-Down Dinner, Family Style—For more informal gatherings, everyone takes their seats and massive platters of food are set in the centers of the tables. Everyone takes what they wish, and they pass the platters around.

Catered At-Home with Servers—Just because the party's at your place doesn't mean you have to skip the caterer's menu . . . or the waiters serving your guests. You can arrange for both in the comfort of your own home.

Catered At-Home with Stations—You'll be at home, but you'll set up a lavish buffet with separate food stations where guests can fix their own pasta plates, salad plates, sushi dishes, kebab choices, seafood picks, and so on.

Dessert and Champagne Party—It could be at home or in a hotel ballroom, in a hotel suite or on the terrace overlooking a golf course or beach. The difference for this evening event is that the entire menu is made up of cake and a wide array of desserts from mousses to tartlets, eclairs to chocolate-covered strawberries, bananas Foster to key lime pie, even trays of cookies or cupcakes for the kids if you like. A formal party, champagne is the drink of choice and the word of the day is *decadence.*

Casual Cookout—It's a barbecue in the backyard, with a better than hot dogs menu. Fire up some ribs, filet mignons wrapped with bacon, rosemary-wrapped corn, portabello mushrooms, short ribs, and put out a spread of great salads and cold choices like clams on the half-shell, king crab legs, or vegetarian quiches and carrot slaw with raisins. Choose a menu that's unique, gourmet, and unlike anything others have served in their backyards.

Clambake on the Beach—Everyone's barefoot in the sand, and the fire is roaring. You'll serve clams, lobster tails, corn on the cob, baked potatoes, greens, and a great micro-brew for this casual beachside gathering.

A Picnic—Colorful blankets set on the lawn create that wonderful "how life used to be" scene that today's kids might find amazing. Picnic baskets set at each blanket contain great sandwiches, unique spreads and crackers, grissini, grapes, garlic bread, and soft drinks like iced tea and lemonade. Copy the menu you shared on one of your first picnic dates, to share this memory with your guests.

Brunch—The spread is amazing at the hotel brunch. Enjoy the free mimosas and coffee and dig into that crème brûlée French toast, crispy bacon, smoked salmon tray, or custom-made omelets. The menu is diverse, and the natural mingling style of a brunch means that your single female guests could time their approach to the petit four tray at the perfect time to chat up your attractive single nephew. You know how to make matchmaking moments happen.

Tea—Think of yourselves as already being in Bermuda or in London, where tea is served in the afternoon with a selection of scones, cakes, shortbreads, and finger sandwiches.

Wine and Cheese Party—You won't get through the night without someone mentioning his or her favorite Pinot, and all wine enthusiasts will sip to their heart's content as they pick on amazing gourmet spreads of fruits, cheeses, and stuffed Bries, salamis and hot hors d'oeuvres, fondues, and grape platters. It's an elegant, classy party and a celebration of your "good year" as well.

Ethnic Theme—With a theme set to honor your heritage, the reception could be a buffet of cultural foods (all identified on printed cards, of course) or chef-prepared meals that are a performance in themselves. Your celebration becomes an education too, as food rituals are enacted, new tastes are shared, your world travels celebrated when you can tell about how you tried vegemite during your trip to Australia or kimchi in South Korea. Make it an international night, if you wish, celebrating all the cultures you've visited during your years together.

Family Holiday Tradition—Or, you could turn your family's traditional Thankgiving dinner into your renewal celebration, with an extra reason to have a second helping of pumpkin pie.

Destination Event Style—If you're flying everyone to Hawaii for a destination celebration, your reception could be a local island style, such as a luau complete with hula dancing and fire baton twirling while you spoon up your poi and hand over the mai tais to your guests.

Your Location Can Inspire Your Style

Some locations are just meant for a certain type of celebration. An estate home with gorgeous gardens, for instance, is the perfect setting for a *Great Gatsby*–type party with cocktails served poolside and white fabric lengths dancing in the breeze from the tent. A winery invites a stylish and sophisticated event, a traveling party with a hot hors d'oeuvres buffet in the tasting room and then an al fresco dinner served on tables set on the beautiful grounds among the grape arbors.

When you're looking at locations, perhaps considering your home or yard rather than trekking to the nearest winery, think about the style of celebration that comes to mind. What do you imagine for your backyard? A tent? Adirondack chairs placed around your willow trees? A stage set up in the corner by the fence for the keyboardist and guitar player? Do you see a table draped with a white tablecloth holding chafing dishes from your favorite restaurant?

If you're looking at a restaurant's party room and you notice its amazing chandelier, do you think about a *Phantom of the Opera* theme with everyone dressed formally, great champagne, and the soundtrack from that musical playing as guests fill the dance floor?

Sometimes it's the space you're in that can deepen your celebration style dreams ("I want *lots* of candles on those great windowsills overlooking the mountains!"), or perhaps even convince you that you *don't* want a formal wedding do-over, but rather prefer a casual cookout on the beach or at your home with a toast by your fireplace at the end of the evening.

Keep in mind that your location may inspire a style, but you will have to go by the rules of the house. As mentioned earlier, some sites do not allow tents to be set up on their grounds, and others require that you use their caterers. Some have strict space limits, allowing only forty guests, and others do not allow alcohol. Many couples have had their celebration style arrive after a long process of elimination: the sites they looked at had too many parameters, too many limits. Too large, too small, too ornate, too plain. When the place is wrong, the "if only" inspiration that was stymied there will ultimately lead you to the right location where your wished-for style can evolve.

TERRY AND T. J. JANKOWSKI, MARRIED SEPTEMBER 7, 1975,
RENEWED SEPTEMBER 16, 2005

"As a transplant survivor, I wanted to celebrate the most wonderful things in my life. My husband is a very special man, so on the occasion of our thirtieth anniversary, we planned a wedding vow renewal ceremony. We wanted something very simple and relaxed, where our guests would come without gifts. They are our gifts. So we arranged to renew our vows at a restaurant that had a gazebo outside, which we decorated with balloons, streamers, and tulle. Then, we all went into the restaurant for a luncheon with a choice of eggplant parmigiana, chicken parmigiana, or a club sandwich. Afterward, everyone came back to our place for dessert: rice pudding (my recipe, which I made), cheesecake (my daughter's recipe, which she made), ambrosia, sugar-free Jell-O for those who can't have anything else, Italian pastries, and my favorite Portuguese custard cups, all of which we laid out in stations throughout our house. To drink, we served wine, coffee, tea, and cordials. It may sound simple, but it was very special."

14

THE MENU AND CAKE

You have your style of reception in mind, whether it's a sit-down dinner, a cocktail party with passed hot and cold hors d'oeuvres, a wine and cheese buffet served on silver platters, a clambake or barbecue, an ethnic celebration, a brunch, and so on. Now it's time to actually select every delicious item that will be on your menu. Renewal couples tell me that tackling this task was their time to shine. Many of them know their gourmet foods and wines, have traveled the world, and have experienced home entertainers with a mastery in their own kitchens. Planning the menu, for them, was a peak experience in preparing for the party. Many husbands too claim this task as their favorite, experienced as they are with all things culinary.

Knowing that party guests consider the food to be the main attraction at any celebration, a make-or-break element that guests will discuss either for its outstanding or disappointing quality, the big concern among couples planning their own event is that the menu be spectacular.

⟨≋⟩

MARTIE DUNCAN, CELEBRITY WEDDING EVENT COORDINATOR, ON FOOD STATIONS AND BUFFETS

I spoke with Martie Duncan, renowned celebrity wedding coordinator who has advised on *Oprah* wedding specials, the movie *My Best Friend's Wedding* with Julia Roberts and Cameron Diaz, and other stellar wedding events about the hot trends in interactive food stations.

Food stations and buffets are back! The mashed potato bar is a big hit, something surprising that guests love. It's comfort food, where they can choose between several different kinds of mashed potatoes—garlic, chives, rosemary, for instance—and then top it with a variety of choices like a mushroom sauce, gravies, and different kinds of cheeses. The make-your-own-pasta bar has been around for ages, but now it's getting a twist with different kinds of pastas and unique toppings like spinach and seafood. Sushi stations offer a range of customary choices, and a chef can be there to hand-roll your guests' requests. All of the sushi choices may be laid out on an ice platter or cutout to an ice sculpture for added flair. A new and growing trend is called a churrascaria, which originates from Brazilian barbecue or steakhouses. Servers, who are called gauchos, walk around with different types of delicious meats on long skewers and they carve the choice of meat right onto the guest's plate. It's a new spin on the old carving station, interactive and personalized, and guests enjoy the experience as well as the food. The trend in food stations is unique, interactive, personalized, and a twist on a standard.

Let's find your chef or caterer. If you'd rather bring in a pro (and thus not have to worry about prep times, food storage and how in the world you'll heat everything up at the right time without breaking a sweat at the kitchen stove), then this is your starting point.

ALL YOU HAVE TO DO IS ASK

Keep in mind first that with a professional chef or caterer, you'll most likely be presented with an extensive list of the menu choices he or she provides, a categorized checklist of appetizers, entrees, food station choices, and desserts. While that list may be *amazing*, you are free to request items that aren't on the list. Most chefs tell me they're happy to customize dishes for couples who make special requests. They'll combine menu items into combination platters, giving you a twist on surf and turf with a lobster meat in wine sauce and madeira-soaked London broil, or special dietary choices like vegan dishes or organic choices to suit your preferences.

Finding a Great Caterer

Ask all of your recently married friends and family if they can recommend a fantastic chef or caterer for your celebration. The best referral is from personal experience, so ask for suggestions. A wedding coordinator could be your perfect resource, even if he or she is hired only for the task of locating a terrific caterer (or a dozen of them for you to interview).

Another option is looking online through professional chef and caterers' associations to find information on experts near you. Caterers' listings may include their years of experience, any special events they catered, awards they've won, their culinary specialties, even their menus for you to browse. Here are the top associations for you to check:

National Association of Catering Executives: www.nace.net
International Association of Culinary Professionals:
www.iacp.com
International Special Events Society: www.ises.com

For smaller parties, you might wish to hire a personal chef whose menu entices you for its creativity, and also perhaps for ethnic and dietary focus. Check out www.personalchef.com, and follow the newest trend in catering smaller renewal celebrations.

Review caterers' menu choice lists to create a *unique* selection of dishes, with something for everyone to enjoy. Ahead of time, sample a few new selections and you might just discover a crowd-pleasing choice.

Interviewing Chefs and Caterers

Once you find experts who sound terrific, you'll set up appointments to interview them and enjoy their tasting platters. Professional chefs and caterers expect you to request this sit-down meeting where they'll present bite-sized samples of their appetizers, entrees, specialities, sauces, and desserts, so sign up for an enjoyable tasting session. You should ask the following:

- How many years of experience do you have?
- Where did you get your degree or culinary certificate?
- At which restaurants or hotels have you worked?
- Have you won any awards for your work?
- Which culinary specialities do you have?
- Can you create our requested custom menu?
- Do you have a budget menu?
- Do you have vegetarian, kosher, or other special request menus?
- Can we see your inspection and insurance certificates?
- Have you worked at our site before?
- Will you need to rent items to work at our site or will you submit a list of items we'll need to rent?
- Do you work our style of party? (Important: some chefs don't work outdoors or in private homes)
- Will you need to come to our home—or the site—to assess the kitchen and storage areas?

IMPORTANT ISSUES TO DISCUSS WITH YOUR CATERER

You'll need to discuss any food allergy issues, such as requesting that no shellfish or shellfish sauce be used in your menu, and ask the caterer for advice about specialty platters for your guests who are vegans or are under special dietary restrictions (no sodium, for instance). Beyond the danger zone, also discuss the various in-season foods that will be better priced at the time of your party. You might learn about new meat and seafood offerings, seasonal vegetables for unique side dishes, game meats, and other options you hadn't considered. Make great use of the chef's knowledge, and you can customize your menu for less money.

Of course, your main decision on who to hire will revolve around your tasting session, and how impressed you are with the dishes set before you. You deserve the best for your party, and it's all a matter of taste.

Your Favorite Place

Of course, you might not feel the need to hire a professional caterer or chef, but rather wish to have your favorite restaurant cater your party. Perhaps the local Italian eatery has always been your source for family party menus, and it will be no different this time. You know their food is terrific, and you want to include this tradition for your big day. If so, enjoy! Select your longtime favorites off their catering list, and perhaps add on a few new choices. You might even choose to hold your celebration at your favorite family restaurant, and of course, you can cater in from several different family favorites, mixing up your selections for each phase of your celebration.

We'll Just Do All the Cooking

You may, of course, prep all the foods yourselves. You may decide that the very meals you've always prepared with and for each other will comprise your menu. You both get to show off! Bring in additional family members or friends who love to cook (and have offered to help), and the result could be a very enjoyable day spent in the kitchen, sharing a bottle of wine and tasting each other's masterpieces. So many couples report that their "cooking day" was a highlight of the week. Others say they were thrilled to make one or several options for the party, and then cater in all the rest. Family recipes become a part of your event, which adds a marvelous level of personalization. And then of course, there's the interactive-yet-not-exhausting group activity of shopping at Costco for platters of hors d'oeuvres, seafood, sushi, and heat-up entrees—all transferred into serving platters and bowls, a top trend among time-crunched renewal couples who have discovered great food options at their neighborhood bulk buy shop. Another option is to fill your party menus with choice items from a gourmet supermarket like King's, Genuardi's, Trader Joe's, or even at a healthy food shop like Whole Foods Market for organic salads, entrees, meats, cheeses, soups, and desserts. The stores' chefs do all the heavy lifting, and you just heat everything up. Couldn't be easier.

Wines and Drinks

Wines

Just as important as planning your menu is arranging an outstanding collection of wines and drinks to please the sophisticated palate. One of the biggest trends in entertaining today is offering a selection of amazing, perhaps award-winning vintages. With the help of a wine shop keeper or by researching online wine sites, you'll find that pairing the perfect vintages with your chosen dishes is an art form. Serve a sour wine and your celebration goes flat. But offer a fantastic new find, and your guests will be raving and asking you where you found the bottle. The same goes for champagnes.

The premiere source for all things in wines and champagnes, including the best-rated wines in a range of price categories is www.winespectator.com. Here, you'll find the latest news and vintage descriptions, winery histories and even travel news for wine-tasting tours and trips. You'll find wine and food pairing suggestions customized to your choices of entrees and appetizers, and even desserts (check out Australian "stickies," a category of dessert wine that's raising cheers across the globe). Find out where the best new wines are hailing from: Argentina, New Zealand, South Africa, the south of France, Mendocino, Napa, Sonoma, Tuscany and so on.

Look into wine blends, and sign up for wine-tastings at your local gourmet wine shop to try dozens of unique vintages to pair to your menu or hold a wine-tasting party at home to sample the possibilities before you shop for your party. When you experiment, you may find that you prefer one vintage above all others and will serve that as your house red or house white. While you can stock up on a large range of wines for your event, as you might with a formal renewal celebration, for your less formal party lay in a simpler selection of two or three different great-tasting wines that work well with your chosen menu.

Champagne

A fine champagne toast might be on your wishlist, so check out the finest champagne your budget allows. For some couples, it's worth spending a few hundred dollars on fine bottles of champagne. Their relationship deserves no less than the best. What matters most is quality, the smoothness of the taste, and perhaps a sentimental effect: you'll serve the same champagne you served at your wedding (or perhaps the champagne you *wish* you could have served at your wedding).

One serving style in champagne is dressing up your champagne. Add a few splashes of pomegranate juice and a sprinkling of pomegranate seeds, or peach juice, strawberry juice, or a single strawberry or raspberry at the bottom of each champagne flute. A little dash of color adds a lovely hue to your champagne toast, and color-coordinating your drink to your color scheme is a popular practice right now.

Again, check www.winespectator.com for the latest news in champagnes and sparkling wines (the technical term for champagnes that do not come from the Champagne region of France).

Mixed Drinks

If you'll provide a full bar at your celebration, think about the types of drinks you'd like to serve. You could build your bar around a selection of popular party drinks or limit the choices to just two or three different types of mixed drinks to simplify and to keep your budget in check.

To help you decide on your bar menu, whether you're selecting from a restaurant or site's list or shopping for your own party, here are the top mixed drink choices at today's celebrations: martinis (visit www.foodtv.com for a selection of great martini recipes), vodka and mixer drinks such as vodka and cranberry juice or orange juice, gin and tonics, rum and Cokes (for beach parties, try Malibu rum and Diet Coke), mojitos, caipirinhas, daiquiries, margaritas, cosmopolitans, sake drinks, sangrias (check www.foodtv.com for unique sangria recipes, including a white sangria), and for color, try blue Hawaiians or retro pink squirrels.

BEERS AND MICROBREWS

Especially for your clambake or beach party, a backyard barbecue, or other informal gathering, select unique beers, ales, microbrews, cider beers, and perhaps local beers for your guests to try.

After-Dinner Drinks

You might decide to finish off the evening with a collection of after-dinner drinks and hot treats your guests don't get every day. Consider the following: espresso with Sambuca and lemon, cappuccino, Irish coffee, Jamaican coffee, flavored coffees such as hazelnut and almond, cognac, brandy, anisette, Bailey's Irish Cream, Chambord, and dessert wines, such as Australian "stickies" and other varietals.

Nonalcoholic Drinks

We're seeing more renewal celebrations step away from the heavy-drinking style of some weddings, with couples preferring to keep the libations to a minimum. Some couples plan no-alcohol events as both a support to relatives in recovery from drinking problems, and also as a social statement to their kids that alcohol is not necessary to have a great time with family and friends.

Get creative with your nonalcoholic drink and soft drink menus. Come up with great virgin daiquiris, flavored iced teas, unique soft drinks, and even hot white chocolate drinks and spiced or mulled ciders for winter celebrations. The big trend in soft drinks right now is the unique cola. You'll find a selection of artsy bottled colas in unexpected flavors like cranberry, Fuji apple (from www.fizzylizzy.com), blueberry, blackberry, clementine (from www.izze.com), Key lime (www.steaksoda.com), ginger, vanilla crème, black cherry, and from Fentiman's (www.fentimans.com) a Seville orange that could complement your décor colors. Also, check out green tea and white tea iced teas, various fruity iced teas like peach and raspberry, and pure fruit juices like grape, apple, and cranberry.

Provide plenty of add-ins for spring water, juices and seltzers, such as lemons, limes, oranges, pineapple chunks, kiwi slices, cherries, and perhaps even skewered fruit kebabs to add to a glass of water or a frozen daiquiri.

And of course, you can take your crafty nature to your ice cubes, dropping a raspberry, strawberry, or mint leaf into each ice cube tray section for custom "designer" ice cubes at your party. Find great drink stirring sticks at the party supply store or wine shop to dress up your glasses or mugs, rim margarita glasses with salt or colored salt, and check out ordering personalized coasters for your party at the Museum of Modern Art store (www.momastore.org) or Pearl River for Asian-inspired custom coasters (www.pearlriver.com).

Symbolic Drinks

Of course, you can bring in the same types of drinks that have been a part of your love story, such as the vintage of wine you shared on your first date or on a special anniversary, the champagne you toasted one another with on your honeymoon, the white mocha coffee you always have on Sunday mornings. Personalize your drink menu with the tastes of your romantic history and share the stories with your guests on printed cards set up by the bar, perhaps with a photo of the two of you toasting at your wedding or on that honeymoon getaway.

The Cake

You can almost taste it right now, can't you?

Your choice of delectable cake might be an air-light lemon cake with buttercream frosting, a chocolate ganache masterpiece with raspberry sauce and dark chocolate shavings, carrot cake with sweet cream cheese frosting, or a taste-of-home chocolate chip cake with cannoli-cream filling. Name your favorite flavors, and your cake is created. Today's cake bakers work wonders with fabulous flavors, fillings, and frostings, and the plain vanilla cake with strawberries that you may have had at your wedding is now called "retro." Today, you can have a rum cake, a cake created to taste like a Mounds bar, ice cream filling layers, or a different flavor for each layer when you can't choose between passion fruit or lemon. Your cake can look like a traditional wedding cake, complete with white buttercream frosting and piped rosettes, or it can be dark chocolate fudge frosted with a burst of red sugar-paste flowers on the top. It can be a three-tiered bridal shape, or it can be a pyramid . . . or a cake sculpture that looks like the Eiffel Tower, where he originally proposed to you.

Any kind of cake you want . . . you got it. Cake designers are more like cake *artisans* and cake *architects*. The more unique, the better, especially for vow renewal celebrations: There are no rules, after all. You don't need to choose from a list of acceptable flavors and fillings, colors or shapes. Or, you could choose to have the most traditional, most glorious five-tiered sugar-paste-flower–covered bridal cake masterpiece anyone in your family has ever seen. If you're doing-over your wedding, and you didn't get to choose your cake (your parents picked it out) or you didn't have the budget for a fantasy wedding cake back then, now you can make your wedding cake fantasy come true. Several renewal couples say they devoted a huge portion of their renewal celebration budgets to their cakes, just so they could have that moment back again. Some recreated their original wedding cake—same flavor, same filling, same cake topper.

First, how many cakes do you want? This is another top trend. You might choose not to have one giant majestic cake on a special cake table, but rather a half dozen *smaller* cakes of different shapes and styles, each placed in the center of your guest tables (with your own on your table, of course). You'll then get to choose multiple styles and flavors or identical cakes of your chosen design. It's up to you. The smaller mini-cakes, if you will, allow your guests to help themselves, and they even promote mingling when your guests visit other tables for a taste of their Key lime or white chocolate cake with mocha sauce.

Cake Flavors

Perhaps when you were first married, there were no options. It might have been that your family's tradition, or your baker's choice, was the traditional bridal white cake with strawberry filling and white frosting. Cakes back then were only personalized by their toppers, not their flavors. Everyone's was the same. Now that you're older, wiser, more cultured, and the world of cakes has expanded to unique tastes (including coffee flavors, habañero peppers, and edible flowers), your options are virtually unlimited.

Beyond the usuals of vanilla, lemon, and chocolate cake, today's wedding vow renewal couples are asking for unique choices like pineapple coconut, espresso-soaked, chocolate mousse, passion fruit, cannoli cream, chocolate truffle, cheesecake, banana mousse, Kahlúa fudge rum or Grand Marnier mousse, white chocolate buttercream, and berry mousse.

YOUR FAVORITE ICE CREAM

You can order or make your cake filled with your favorite ice cream flavor, such as Godiva White Chocolate Raspberry or Ben & Jerry's Chunky Monkey or Chubby Hubby. It's a top trend right now in both renewal ceremonies and weddings to bring in a shared favorite snack, that taste of home, or a bite with a story to it, such as "We always eat Cherry Garcia on our anniversary, as a wink to how we went out for ice cream on our first date."

For frostings, you have your choice of many. Traditional buttercream frosting holds up the best in warm weather, such as at your outdoor event, and the following options provide a taste treat: rolled fondant, mocha buttercream, white chocolate, lemon cream, coconut cream. Flowers and fruits may be hand-shaped using sugar-paste icing, royal icing, or marzipan, so ask your baker about those beautiful cake accents that he or she can use to decorate your cake.

Coffee and Liqueur Soaks

If you're among the couples who wish to add a dash of liqueur to the cake, perhaps as part of your champagne and dessert party, think about the following most popular choices: rum-, espresso- or, cappuccino-flavored, Grand Marnier, Kahlúa, Frangelico, and Chambord.

As an extra treat, consider offering a selection of decadent sauces that guests can pour or drizzle onto their cake slices: chocolate fudge, white chocolate, raspberry, lemon, vanilla, caramel, berry, and hot apple and cinnamon.

Your Cake Topper

The most popular topper for vow renewal cakes is the original cake topper from your wedding. If you've kept and preserved yours, it's time to pull it out and perhaps have it cleaned and spruced up to use again on your new cake. In instances where the cake topper was the traditional bride and groom figurines, it's now considered retro to use them again. Of course, you could choose to upgrade your Mini-Mes, as today's versions found in craft stores, bakeries, and online come in a wide range of personalized styles and skin colors, a range of hairstyles, and of course you can order customized figures that look just like you.

If you'd rather top this cake with something nonbridal and unique, as many brides and grooms are doing, you can choose from the following:

- Sprays of unique flowers stuck into the top cake layer
- A tiara, set with either rhinestones or faux gemstones
- Sugar-paste flowers in your choice of size and flower style (one couple chose sugar-paste birds of paradise for their tropical island getaway celebration)
- Fruits
- A chocolate figurine, either dark or white chocolate, in the shape of something personalized to your relationship (for instance, chocolate cellos and violins for musician couples)

- A bell (symbolizing the wedding bell, this one might be crystal or sterling silver or made from spun sugar)
- Silk flowers or doves bought at the craft store and perched atop your cake
- Fun, playful pinwheels for your whimsical, outdoor, casual celebration
- A ceramic lighthouse from the craft store
- A faux starfish, propped up on a bed of icing, for your beach celebration

Cupcakes

Even celebrities are choosing cupcakes in place of traditional circular or sheet cakes. It's a fun trend that's easy to arrange.

Either make them with a team of helpers—which is the usual scenario—or order them from your bakery. Use color-coordinated paper or foil cupcake wrappers, choose from the flavor and icing suggestions on the previous pages, and these tasty little cakes are ready for your party. You can serve them on silver platters or pile them up on circular platforms easily made out of concentric Styrofoam circles from the craft store and covered with a great arrangement of fabric.

You can personalize your cupcakes with such choices as mini chocolate chips, white chocolate chips, peanut butter chips, shredded coconut, M&M's, rainbow-colored sprinkles, mini peanut butter cups, jelly beans, preformed sugar-paste flowers from www.gailwatsoncakes. com, a flower rosette in colored icing made using a pastry bag, or a single mini chocolate monogram initial (get these at your local chocolate candy shoppe).

Additional Desserts

What about apple pie à la mode? That's one of the top choices of vow renewal couples who want that taste of home either in place of or in addition to a cake. Dessert options have gotten *fun*, and couples are personalizing their menus with unexpected choices. Other dessert options might be Boston cream pie, oversized cream puffs smothered with whipped cream, crème brûlée, lemon meringue pie, Napoleans with unique fruit toppings, cheesecake, white chocolate mousse, pumpkin pie and pecan pie, carrot cake, or chocolate fondue with cubes of pound cake, chocolate chip pound cake, cookies, and fruit.

The Dessert Bar

Taking a cue from those formal events where food stations offer amazing options, dessert stations or dessert bars allow guests to prepare their own customized desserts. You'll provide the basics, plus a dozen or so topping possibilities. Consider the following for your bar theme, with a variety of toppings at the ready: ice cream, gelato, chocolate mousse, pudding, Italian ice, milkshakes, hot fruit crepes, and ice cream sandwiches.

And then there's the chocolate fountain. I've saved the hottest trend for last, and this one is picking up steam. Imagine a gorgeous fountain, only it's warm, rich dark liquid chocolate flowing down from each tier. You'll have your choice of skewered bites ready for a chocolate coating: strawberries, macaroons, pound cake squares, rum cake squares, cherries, chocolate cake squares, and brownie squares (in case you just can't get enough chocolate). This interactive feature is not only fun for guests to use, it fills the room with the intoxicating scent of chocolate.

JENNIFER AND GREG GRIZZLE, MARRIED OCTOBER 19, 1991,
RENEWED OCTOBER 19, 1996

"We invited six couples to join us on our getaway wedding vow renewal celebration in Las Vegas, and since they traveled so far to be with us, we wanted to show them a great time. So we took them to all the tacky, touristy places Vegas is famous for. But the best part of the 'entertainment' at our event was the Elvis officiant we hired. We had our choice between a young Elvis and a seventies Elvis, and everyone loved the seventies Elvis we selected. While he took the vows part seriously, he broke into song, he danced, he strutted up and down the aisle, he added funny things like 'don't step on my blue suede shoes' to the ceremony. Everyone was laughing so hard, it made for a very memorable and very entertaining celebration. Afterward, we took our guests out for a sit-down dinner and dancing, but it was the Elvis officiant that everyone loved."

15

THE ENTERTAINMENT

The entertainment you have at your celebration is another one of those areas that depends on the formality, size, style, and location of your event. After all, you wouldn't have a twelve-piece orchestra at a small gathering for fifteen guests. You wouldn't spin your own CDs at a formal ballroom event with 250 guests in attendance. So think about what fits the scope of your celebration.

Formal events like a wedding do-over, for instance, open up the option of auditioning bands and DJs, just as first-time brides and grooms are doing for their weddings. Many couples whose vow renewal ceremony is the chance to have the wedding they never had, on a larger budget than they originally had, and with full freedom to create the extravagant day of their dreams, are looking for that twelve-piece band . . . and perhaps a few extra soloists and pianists for their cocktail hour.

At slightly less formal events, either at a hotel ballroom, restaurant, winery, or at home, couples are still bringing in musicians. Maybe not a nine-piece band, but often a smaller ensemble like a keyboardist and guitarist who perform delightfully. Singers, jazz trumpeters, pianists, and cellists are popular options for cocktail parties and dessert and champagne celebrations, and pianists may already be in place at a hotel's upscale brunch.

Informal parties, like a backyard gathering, might be the perfect place for a friend to play the guitar as the opening act of your celebration. Or you can play your favorite music CDs (more on that in a moment), or just set the radio to your favorite soft rock or party song station. Fun-loving couples have been known to rent karaoke machines for some laughs and cheers as their friends and family perform. Don't forget that karaoke machines come with kids' song tracks too, inviting the little ones to play along. This is the kind of relaxed atmosphere that can open up opportunities for unforgettable entertainment that doesn't cost a fortune.

Make Your Own Music

The number one trend in entertainment for vow renewal ceremonies and receptions is creating your own collection of songs. With the ease of CD burners and MP3s comes the fun task of creating your own soundtrack. Beyond dining-appropriate music and songs from paradise, you can include all of the songs that have meant the most to you over the years. With the help of your kids, if you need it, you can go song-by-song through your own CD collection, adding to your playlist your favorite songs from your long history together, the song you first slow-danced to, the song that was playing when you got engaged, the soundtrack of your lives together.

As an added perk, you can make copies of your playlist CD and give them out to your guests as keepsakes or favors from the event.

You can also choose the music for your ceremony's processional, interlude, and recessional—all on one CD with a friend instructed to hit the play button at the right time. This allows you access to beautiful songs in the original artists' recordings, like George Winston's "Summer" or a lilting arrangement of Vivaldi's *Four Seasons*. These two are among the top choices for ceremony soundtracks.

For your reception, you might create two different CDs: one for the dinner hour, featuring slower-tempo music or dining music such as Michael Bublé's vocals or Chris Botti's trumpet performances, perhaps jazz music or movie soundtrack songs.

If you'll have dancing at your reception, your CD mix will include your favorite faster songs, party favorites, Motown songs, or collections from your favorite artists. You know your guests and what music style will get them out on the dance floor, whether it's eighties music, ethnic songs, or Glenn Miller Orchestra big band.

Not in the mood to mix your own CDs? You can use movie soundtrack CDs for collections of great songs or just pull out your own favorite CDs from your home collection. One couple tells me they used their own collection of jazz CDs. Over the years, they've always gone to great jazz clubs for dinner and live entertainment, and they often purchased the artists' CDs at the end of the night. Now, for their renewal celebration, they already had their play list ready to go, and as a bonus it reflected their favorite times spent together.

Personal Showcase

Another big trend at wedding vow renewal services and receptions is the personal showcase, such as when your granddaughters choreograph and perform a song for you. It might be a number from their dancing school class (imagine the little ones in their costumes performing for all of your guests), or an act they plan for you on their own (creative little artists that they are). Perhaps your father will play the guitar for you, like he did at your wedding, or your friends will sing a karaoke song in your honor.

Live Entertainment

If you're wrinkling your nose at the idea of playing CDs at your celebrations, and instead wish to have live entertainment, this section is for you . . .

Before we get to the quintessential question of DJ versus band for your entertainment, consider having *different* types of entertainers, which many couples find to be the perfect, unique choice to set their celebration apart from a traditional wedding and still give guests an experience to remember.

Imagine a harpist playing lilting songs at your renewal ceremony, or a flutist playing as the two of you approach the altar. Imagine a pianist playing in the background during your brunch reception, or an acoustic guitarist strumming and singing songs during your dinner hour. The addition of live musical performers can be the perfect special touch to your day.

If you do wish to hire a musical performer for all or part of your event (you could, for instance, hire the harpist just for your ceremony), you'll start out by searching for qualified performers. You might check with local universities or schools for the arts, where amazingly gifted performers are training for professional life (and could use a paying gig), or get the card of that great guitarist playing at the coffee shop or bookstore. Or, you could check with a musicians' association in your area. There might be a group of professional musicians and performers who have banded together (sorry for the pun) in order to be found by clients like you. At sites like these, you'll discover the details and repertoires of musicians like harpists, cellists, pianists, organists, trumpeters, and groups like trios and quartets, with background information on the performers and links to their own Web sites where you may find audio and video samples of their shows.

Once you find your potential performers, you can set up an audition and interview in order to experience their talent. If possible, see them performing live, such as at a concert or hotel brunch (a favorite spot of mine to find fabulous pianists), as an audio- or videotape might not convey their performing style and presence quite as well.

You're not limited to hiring just one musician or singer. You might choose one for your ceremony, or a pair such as a pianist and singer. Then, for your reception, you can have a salsa band or the jazz trio.

GOING ETHNIC

Don't forget about ethnic associations, where you'll find the names and contact information for a range of ethnic and cultural performers. A mariachi band, steel drum band, bagpipers, African drummers, klezmer groups, Italian opera singers, or Irish tenors.

Questions to ask:
- How long have you been performing?
- What's your musical training? Did you attend a school or university for the arts?
- Do you play any other instruments? Would you be willing to play both during our event?
- Have you performed at many weddings or special event parties?
- What are your prices and time limit packages? Your overtime fees?
- Do you charge for travel?
- What will you wear to our event?

A DJ or a Band

The choice between a DJ or a band is often a matter of budget, as bands usually cost more than DJs due to the presence of multiple band members. But it's also a matter of style and what you envision for your party. Are you picturing a live band in suits, complete with a crooner and a bass player who can dance? Do you love the idea of a live performance by a band, with the lead singer interacting with your guests, perhaps a line of trumpeters blasting out the Latin music you love? Or perhaps you'd rather hear original-artist versions of your favorite songs, as a DJ would play, and not someone else's version. Perhaps you love the idea of a six-piece orchestra in tuxedoes or a swing band in zoot suits, a USO-type band with Andrews Sisters–type singers . . . something unique and exciting for your guests.

Whatever your wish, you'll find these professionals through referrals from recently married friends and family, or friends who have experience planning corporate parties and events (those corporate party planners have *tons* of great contacts). You're welcome at bridal showcases, where bands and DJs work their acts in front of several hundred brides- and grooms-to-be. Your other wedding vendors (like your florist and your caterer) have been in the business for a long time, so they know the good performers from the bad and can often recommend the name of the best jazz trio they've ever seen. And of course, you could hire a wedding coordinator to round up the best options.

You'll observe their show, ask about their price packages and time limits, find out about how long they've been performing and if they've worked any special events lately. If the governor just invited them to play his holiday party, for instance, the odds are that they're good and have a tremendous reputation in your area. Get a personal sense from these performers. How do they interact with you? How do they interact with a crowd? The best performers have a spark about them. They engage their audience with a sense of charm or a natural wit, great banter or jokes that seem natural, not forced or off-color. You'll find out what they'll be wearing to your event, as some performers have a repertoire of outfits and costumes, not just songs.

You'll sign a detailed contract and work with your DJ or band to create a play list, songs you'd like to hear during your celebration . . . as well as your No list for songs you don't want played at all. As one couple put it, "No line dances, no chicken dance, no hokeypokey, and no rap music." You're free to hand over a No Play list, which might include the wedding song of your recently divorced son or daughter or any other songs or artists you object to. It's your party, so you get to make these decisions.

Special Spotlight Dances

No doubt, the greatest entertainment of the day will be the two of you dancing to "your" song. Just as you did at your wedding reception, you'll take to the dance floor for a spotlight dance. Perhaps you're a more graceful pair now, with years of dancing together polishing your skills. Perhaps you're not as shy as you were then. You may relish the attention, when once you blushed from it. Your friends and family look on as you dance to the music, and they'll wonder what you're whispering in each other's ears.

While most couples do choose to dance again to the same song as their wedding's first spotlight dance, there's a new trend afoot: starting off dancing to the first part of that song, and then switching to a *new* song, one that reflects your partnership now. It's incredibly symbolic, the transition from then to now.

THE PIANO BROTHERS SAY . . .

I spoke to Tim and Ryan O'Neill, internationally renowned pianists who have sold over a million CDs and performed at hundreds of weddings and special celebrations like yours. Here is what the Piano Brothers have to say about your song:

Playing tunes from a couple's original ceremony is a wonderful way to tie into the past. People associate specific songs with particular times or events in their lives. And hearing those songs, even ten or twenty years later, can evoke a sense of nostalgia that's even stronger than flipping through a photo album. We also suggest that couples introduce a new song into the vow renewal ceremony, a symbol of their renewed love for each other. By incorporating music from both their past and their present, they're acknowledging every step they took to get them to this point—as well as all the time they'll spend dancing together in the future.

Our top five recommended marriage renewal songs include:

1. "True Companion," Marc Cohn
2. "To Make You Feel My Love," Billy Joel
3. "Always," Ella Fitzgerald
4. "At Last," Etta James
5. "Grow Old Along With Me," John Lennon

Check out Resources for more on song lyric sites and Tim and Ryan O'Neill.

Keep in mind that your spotlight dance doesn't have to resemble your first dance at all. While you may have swayed back and forth in a romantic spin around the dance floor back then, perhaps you're up for a tango this time. Many couples sign up for dance lessons now to prepare for their celebrations. You may decide that it would be tremendous fun for the two of you as well! It can be something new to learn together, and a fun new social activity. Plus, you'll impress your guests, and share a little more about your passion for one another with a significantly spicier dance. (Just keep it clean in front of the kids, okay?) Add a few dips, twirls, and turns, and your spotlight dance is all the more fun to watch. And to share with each other.

(♥)

WHERE TO TAKE DANCE LESSONS

Check online for local dancing lesson studios near you, and be sure to ask for referrals from recently married friends and relatives. You can check the Web sites of the dancing school you know the kids or grand-kids attend. Some dance instructors offer adult classes at night and on weekends.

Other Special Spotlight Dances

You're not the types to hog the spotlight, so consider asking your kids or parents to join you on the dance floor for the second half of your song, or for a slow song played right after that one. You might dedicate a separate song later in the night for your kids to dance to, or dance *with* your children. Father can dance with his daughters, Mother can dance with the sons. Or all you "girls" can dance to a fast song together.

Family song dedications are also popular to have at vow renewal ceremonies. It's a fun way to honor the special people in your life, especially if you're stepping out of your usual comfort zone to dance to a song that your kids or grandkids love. And younger renewal couples might honor their older relatives with a dedication song—and shared dance floor. They may dance to their parents' or grandparents' weddings songs, in a great homage to a family legacy of successful partnerships.

Dedicating songs to one another is a fabulous gift and a moment you'll both love. Choose songs that speak of your feelings for each other now, what you mean to each other, songs that say it all. Open with a short speech inviting your sweetheart to the dance floor and sharing the meaning this song has for you. Such as "This was the song that was playing when we returned from our honeymoon. She was unpacking, and she had no idea I was watching her. I was thinking, 'Wow . . . she's really my wife now. I must have done something really good along the way to deserve a woman like her.' Now, twenty years later, honey, will you dance with me to the very same song?"

Video Presentation

A new and popular feature at renewal celebrations is sharing a video compilation of your greatest times together. Think of those video montages that they show during the Oscar awards program. Beautiful music is playing, and scenes from movies or an actor's life are seamlessly edited to provide a stirring overview of spotlight moments. With a video presentation of your own, you too can add an element of star power to your reception entertainment. The lights dim, and the show begins . . .

You can easily arrange to have a video presentation created for you. Either a talented friend with knowledge of his or her computer's editing software can blend your footage together perfectly—with soundtrack and captions or titles—or you can hire a professional videographer to edit your still photos and home movies into the perfect feature. Your part, if you're not actually the one producing and editing your video segment, is to outline the order in which you'd like your photos and videos to be shown and to provide any titles or wording you'd like to accompany the "chapters" of your life and love story. You can also record a voice-over with *you* telling the story of your partnership. Once edited, your video presentation can be burned onto a DVD or VHS tape and shown during your party or at the start of your vow renewal ceremony. It's your choice.

You can use your wedding footage or ask a friend with a videocamera to capture you in scenes you'd like to create *now* for this video presentation. It might be of the two of you relaxing by the fireplace or walking hand-in-hand along the beach, or funny segments that perfectly personalize your relationship (he's sitting in the den watching the ballgame, while you're trying to get his attention, or he's out masterfully working the barbecue grill and you're chopping mangoes for the chutney).

Just make sure you haven't produced a video segment that's as long as the Oscar awards ceremony. Keep it short and simple, ten minutes tops. Edited well, that's all you'll need. You can, of course, create *two* video presentation products. One is the shorter version to be shown at your event, and the other is a longer version that makes for a perfect family keepsake. Call it your Director's Cut, complete with extra scenes and a blooper reel.

The result is a wonderful experience for all of you, the chance to dance back through your memories, share how wonderful your life together has been, make your guests laugh with your creativity, and of course spotlight your best moments together.

ANNE MARIE JARKA-HAJJAR AND DAN HAJJAR, MARRIED MAY 5, 1990,

RENEWED MAY 5, 2000

"In hindsight, getting married is never easy, but I was so in love that I didn't even think about it. Yet, at twenty-four, with nearly 300 guests—including my husband's newly graduated college roommates as guests and attendants, my three younger sisters and cousins as bridesmaids, and a ticket to transport me from my well-established job into the world of the military, with an overseas tour, no less—I guess I should forgive myself for being nervous, and for not thoroughly enjoying the fabulous party my parents gave me.

"Well, we survived the move, the military, Desert Storm, and a move back. It was challenging but we were better as people and as a couple for having weathered the 'storm.' Things worked in our favor, and the more they did, the more we wanted to give. We started mentoring kids and eventually, a few months before our ten-year wedding anniversary, Dan and I decided that if God would allow it, we wanted to expand our family of two to a family of three. It was a time to rejoice, and in celebration we decided to formally renew our vows.

"Our original priest was available and instead of my sisters and cousins, our nieces and godchildren served as the 'wedding party.' We opted to replace our original centerpieces, a single open white rose floating in a crystal bowl, with three open white roses. After all, we were celebrating our past, our present, and our future! We dressed dolls in our original attire and wrote personal notes on each program. Our invitation said,

Come one, Come all,
    to our anniversary Ball.
Come celebrate love and romance,
    with food, drink and dance!
It is our way of saying thanks
    to our friends and family.
We hope to see you there,
    Love, Dan and Anne Marie

"It was a glorius event! Much more intimate than the first pass—and many, many more positive, 'in the moment' memories for me! I think my friend summed up the experience best: 'When you attend a wedding you are hoping the relationship will survive. Being part of a celebration for a couple ten years later . . . well . . . you are truly celebrating a success!' There are no guarantees, but renewing our vows in the way that we did helped to reconfirm the commitments we made to each other. We revisited and renewed our love, our friendship, and our passion. And, thanks to God, fourteen months later, our family was indeed expanded to three!"

16

DÉCOR AND CENTERPIECES

Whether you have one table to accent with a beautiful centerpiece or fifty tables for your do-over bash, you have amazing choices both from the world of bridal décor and way, way beyond it. We'll get to centerpiece décor in a moment, but first I'd like to share the latest trends in special décor for renewal celebrations. Since this is a new celebration of the marriage vows you took long ago, you have tremendous and sentimental options to use items and photos from your original wedding right here in your vow renewal celebration.

You can add a personalized touch to your décor by arranging a spotlit table that's dedicated to the artifacts of your original wedding. Guests can browse your collection much as they would do a special showcase at the Louvre or the Smithsonian. You'll arrange this table to show off your own wedding keepsakes, pairing each item with a printed note explaining the item's significance to you both. Here's what might go on the table:

- Your wedding portrait, either in its original silver frame as displayed in your home, or a new enlarged version set on an art easel with a spotlight affixed up top.
- A collection of framed photos featuring the special moments of your life together, such as that first photo of the two of you holding your newborn daughter, family vacation photos, the two of you standing in front of your newly purchased first home.
- Copies of your original wedding program from the wedding day.
- Those matchbooks and printed napkins you had ordered for your wedding reception.
- The guest book from your wedding.

- Your wedding-day garter and handkerchief.
- The ring box that once held your engagement ring, or your wedding rings.
- Your bridal bouquet, if you've had it preserved in a special museum-quality curio box.
- Your original ring pillow.

Make this collection stand out more by accenting the items with well-placed nosegay bouquets or bud vases displaying a single rose or stephanotis bunch. After all, as your note can share, these were the original types of flowers in your bridal bouquet.

Moving Décor
Some couples are borrowing from celebrity wedding events and the Oscar parties by setting up a television (plasma screen optional) set to run their original wedding video or new video presentation. Another option is running DVD footage of scenery that fits the theme of the party, such as underwater footage of sea life or a tropical island vista.

Additional Décor Ideas

Before we get to your centerpieces, think about incorporating some special décor touches that make the most of your environment.

At Home
- Light the fireplace for ambiance
- Set out beautiful pillar candles on decorative holders
- Hang nosegay bouquets on all the doorknobs
- Set out pretty floral centerpieces in your restrooms
- Set out family photos for all to enjoy
- Scatter rose petals on your serving and guest tables

In a Restaurant or Ballroom

The ideas for your home décor will work just as well here, with the addition of:

- Bringing in potted trees and branch trees to give the indoor room an outdoor look.
- Choose a unique ice sculpture. Ice sculptures are making a comeback, as today's ice artists are creating new and unique, personalized masterpieces.
- Use a lot of greenery in your décor. Less expensive than floral arrangements, a great selection of greens set around the room gives a natural, outdoorsy look to your setting. Talk to your floral designer about the great options in unique green fillers plus green versions of calla lilies (very classic).
- Talk to the lighting manager about arranging their existing spotlights and pinlights to aim directly onto your head table, your memento table, or your guests' tables. You might even arrange for a spotlight on your cake. In today's world of special events, the lighting director has become very important. Lighting can transform a room, whether it's with strings of white lights set around a dance floor or custom-created gobo lights that you will order to display your names in lights on the dance floor. (Gobo lights are specially-made metal disk templates that slide into a light projector, shining your choice of words, patterns or pictures onto any surface, even pool surfaces.) Talk to your site manager about a chat with their lighting experts.

At Outdoor Events

- Decorate an existing trellis with green garlands and dramatic flowers
- Spruce up your existing landscape with freshly potted flowers
- If you'll be at poolside, set out floating candles or floating floral wreaths
- Add strings of white lights (called fairy lights or twinkle lights) to the outside eaves of your home, handrails, around the outside edges of tents, in the trees, in landscaping, and along fences

- Set out hurricane lamps with colorful candles inside
- Turn on any fountains or water features you might have, like a koi pond with a waterfall
- Turn on the underwater lights in your pool to give it a great blue glow

A NEW CHUPPAH ALTERNATIVE

Casey Cooper of Botanicals (www.botanicalschicago.com) suggests a unique twist on the chuppah. If you married in a Jewish ceremony, you and your husband stood beneath a chuppah, which symbolized the house you would build as a family. Your parents stood by you during that original ceremony. Now, for your vow renewal, you can stand beneath a grove of trees and tie up a colorful square of organza fabric in a fabulous color—a green or paprika, perhaps. You'll stand beneath this symbolic chuppah, together with your kids perhaps, in a tribute to the house and home you've built together as a family. Decorate with florals and blooms, greenery as you wish, and you'll personalize this fabric chuppah alternative, keeping it afterward as a memento of your big day.

Choosing Your Centerpiece Design

Of course, with the perfect floral centerpieces on each of your tables, you might not need (or want) more décor. I'm a big proponent of avoiding overkill, and sometimes the most lovely and elegant look is minimalist in nature. You may even find that you don't need centerpieces at all for your classic cocktail party, but would prefer a single votive candle in the centers of your tables. Or, the hotel or restaurant where you're holding your celebration already has plans to place bud vases with flowers or candles at the centers of your tables. The details may already be taken care of by them!

If you do wish to accent the center of your tables beautifully, you have a wide range of options in a wide range of budget levels, from

those $150 elevated, overflowing floral centerpieces to a single garde-
nia floating in a bowl of water, for all of $10.

You've seen beautiful table centerpieces in women's magazines,
home décor magazines, and even bridal magazines if you've been flipping through them for ideas. Floral designers work magic with their
artistic combinations of well-known bridal flowers mixed with unique
blooms no one's ever seen before. The combination of flowers, greenery and even branches and tall stalks for height and drama is a masterpiece waiting to happen. Just as lovely, a low-set, tightly bunched
grouping of roses or tulips in a simpler arrangement, surrounded by votive candles, is an elegant, chic minimalist look.

I spoke with Casey Cooper, principal and master floral designer at
Botanicals in Chicago, and here are the top centerpiece requests that
her vow renewal couples are requesting:

- Simple, painted pink wooden boxes filled with dozens of fruits,
  such as Granny Smith apples adorned with well-placed pink rose
  blossoms. After the event, the apples are donated to a food pantry.
- Tall wrought-iron stands, very ornate, topped with floral arrangements. The height gives a more modest arrangement a more

dramatic look. You can rent these stands from your florist, and many hotels have them on hand as well.

- Whimsical colors and choices, such as gerbera daisies for a bright, playful look.

Nonfloral Ideas

You could skip the floral arrangements and use something unique, and perhaps more affordable, for your centerpiece. Many couples are taking their family photo displays, color photocopying the originals, framing them beautifully, and splitting them up to display several on each table. It promotes mingling while all of your guests wander around to check out those great portraits of you and your family. Just keep any candles a safe distance from them, and perhaps accent them with rose petals scattered on the tablecloths or single roses or gardenias placed in front of each photo.

Celebrity event coordinators are using fruits with accents of nuts and mini flowers for this surprising find from the produce section. Pineapples, of course, could be the focus of your centerpiece, and some beach-based couples are piling up coconuts and accenting with hibiscus flowers.

A collection of wine bottles and trays of grapes (green, red, or black), or platters of cheese and crackers, fill your table centers in the manner of a great restaurant or winery tasting room, and your guests can help themselves to the libations and snacks.

For kids' tables, use games or lunchboxes filled with toys and treats for the little ones. The kids won't appreciate a floral centerpiece, so choose something they can play with or snack on. A tray of kid-friendly finger food often does the trick. A top trend coming in about kid table centerpieces: Etch-a-Sketches are the big draw.

Fabulous Linens

Just a quick word about table linens and chair seat covers, in case your celebration plans lead you away from restaurants and other locations that already supply linens, such as an outdoor or beach wedding where linens must be rented.

The world of linen rentals has come a long way in the past few years. While you once may have had your choice of a dozen colored swatches on a piece of cardboard presented by the site manager, now the options have opened. You can find a wide palette of colors, patterns, and textures. Think about the feel of a shimmery silk overlay to a plain linen table cloth, allowing you to blend your color scheme right there on the table. Think about a pearl-encrusted silk dupioni tablecloth for your cake table. Even stretch fabrics are being used to get a nice, tight fit to your chair backs. No more tying up and tripping over "standard-sized" seat linens during the conga line!

Check with your site manager about their full selection of table linens, and look further if you're presented with the same twelve shades of polyester table covers they showed you fifteen years ago. You can find terrific rental agencies that specialize in table and chair fabrics, unique sizes (such as those for long, rectangular tables rather than traditional circular tables for eight), pearl- and crystal-studded fabrics, shimmery fabrics and more. To find great rental companies in your area, plus full stock lists of linens they can provide, check out www.resourceone.info, and www.contemporarycloth.com. To find a rental specialist near you for both linens and those extras like chairs, china, stemware, and tents, visit www.ises.com or www.ararental.org.

Tabletop Options

If you need to rent china, wineglasses, stemware, flatware, champagne flutes, and other items for your guests' tables, you may be pleasantly surprised at what you can find available for your use these days. Without buying a new set of flatware, you can select from a range of unique designs to give your tabletop an exciting style. Even hotels and restaurants are stocking up on the new designs of square dishes and designer chargers, unique wine goblets and intricate flatware that's out on the market today. Now, dishes, glasses, and forks and spoons have become designer accents!

Check out www.tablewaretoday.com, the site of the trade magazine for all of the department stores, specialty shops, and rental agencies. Here, you'll find out the newest trends in table settings—plates
and platters, wineglasses, utensils, champagne flutes, fun and quirky
martini glasses. You'll also find out about the phenomenal new rush of
formalware created by celebrity fashion designers like Vera Wang and
Kate Spade.

You could, of course, use your own wedding collection of china,
stemware, wineglasses, and silverware, and that's a top choice for couples whose guest lists are smaller for an at-home celebration. Or, also
at home, you can use your wedding china *and* rent additional coordinating pieces that add up to an amazing mix-and-match of old and
new. You've just created another then and now scenario for your décor.
So function meets your changing tastes, plus your budget gets a break
when you have the chance to rent only *half* of what you would have
needed.

Think about your style and formality level, any themes or ethnic
influence, even the setting of your celebration. Square plates with an
Asian influence are a hot choice right now, so would square red plates
look fabulous on your buffet table? Now, color is in. Even for wine goblets, with jewel-toned blues and reds adding to the décor of a color-set
table. Open yourselves up to unique shapes and designs, such as mini
vodka glasses in ice-cream-cone shapes. These glasses have no foot or
base to stand on, but rather sit in a larger bowl of ice shavings. Very
chic. And then there are martini glasses with zigzag or spiral stems,
wineglasses with gold rims, dinner plates featuring your monogram under that amazing lobster crepe or beef medallions.

Enjoy all the options of setting your tables so that *they* become a
key décor point of the room. A prettily designed guest table adds extra
flair to your day, and the unique choices in wineglasses or Chinese
soup spoons show that *you* are a master party planner with a fabulous
sense of style.

TINA TESSINA AND RICHARD SHARRARD, MARRIED MAY 9, 1982, RENEWED MAY 9, 1998, AND PLANNING THEIR TWENTY-FIFTH ANNIVERSARY RENEWAL FOR MAY 9, 2007

Tina Tessina, PhD, and Richard Sharrard have renewed their vows several times, each time on a cruise ship, Tina says, because they couldn't possibly improve upon their on-land wedding day.

"We previously renewed our vows on a world cruise we took in 1998, a special event arranged for those onboard. The theme was medieval-kitsch (lords, knights, and ladies) and included a 'knighting' ceremony for those who had cruised most often. Everyone dressed in whatever medieval-type thing we could throw together from what we'd brought on the cruise. Lots of glittery scarves used as veils and capes. The theater was decorated with heraldic banners, and the ship's entertainment staff, dressed as medieval royalty, conducted the ceremonies.

"Our twenty-fifth anniversary cruise will be in May 2007, and we'll most likely cruise from Florida to Spain, then take a Mediterranean cruise, for a total of three weeks. I expect to have a small group (six to eight people) traveling with us. We usually decorate our cabin door with something we've found in a party shop, suited to the theme. This year, we had holographic heart decorations. We also sneak around and decorate the doors of friends who travel with us, to surprise them."

17

FAVORS

I suggest giving out favors that people can actually use. Nothing cheesy or reminiscent of 1970s proms, like those engraved brandy snifters with your names and the date. Look for favors that play into the theme of the celebration, or something that speaks of your relationship and favorite interests. Your favors should go to another level: your favors come with a purpose . . . sharing the "tools" of your successful relationship.

When you give out favors at a vow renewal celebration, you're also saying "we hope you'll be as happy as we are." There's a level of usefulness in them, and also a level of sentimentality. By that, I mean you're sharing a part of your love story with your guests. For instance, when you give out single pink long-stemmed roses in clear cellophane, a note attached can share the story of how your husband gave you the exact same thing as his first gift to you on your second date. When you give out bottles of Pinot Noir, your note says this was the wine you were drinking when he proposed. And when you give out a book of love poems, your note reminds your guests to keep the poetry and words of love in their relationships as well.

Your favors can be a part of the décor as well, if you place one on each guest's plate, or arrange them artfully as the centerpiece. You can arrange a table by the exit where your favors are displayed, or make it an interactive moment by personally handing out favors to your guests.

A Little Something to Take Home

Edibles

- Godiva chocolates. Choose from those little ballotins of two chocolate hearts, or select something that works with your theme, like little raspberry-filled starfish.
- Bagged candies. Like pouches of M&Ms (which you can have *personalized* by initial or special-choice color at www.mms.com), you can bag a handful of a candy that's part of your love story.
- Sugared almonds. They're a tradition at weddings, with deep historical and ancestral meaning. These confections connote marital happiness, fertility, and financial abundance. You can find these in white pastel solids or multihues at bakeries or in bulk at craft stores, and package them up in tulle pouches or cellophane gift bags tied with a ribbon.
- Nuts. Please, *please* don't make everyone cringe with a note reading "We're just nuts about each other." You have more originality than that! A bag of nuts, like cashews or honey-roasted almonds,

even candied walnuts, is a great favor. Not only does it call to the old world tradition of nuts (and in legend, figs) signifying a good harvest, wealth, and fertility, it could be another tribute to your early dating days. You shared a bag of peanuts at a baseball game, perhaps.

- Sauces and spices. Edibles like these share your love of all things culinary. You love to cook together, to go out to new restaurants, try new ethnic cuisines. It's one of your shared passions. So give out some curry spices or chipotle sauces (check out www.pepper people.com for the best sauces I've found), even a bottle of dessert sauce like the raspberry sauce that was on your engagement dessert.

- Frosted cookies. We're back from the spicy stuff to the sweet stuff with baggies or gift boxes of frosted cookies. Visit www.chery landco.com for a wide variety of frosted cookies and brownies, and of course you can always *make* your own special-recipes cookies, like the double chocolate chunk fudge cookies your kids always request when they come home to you.

- Bottles of wine. It could be the same bottle you shared upon your engagement, the one you have on each anniversary, or a new favorite you found at a restaurant or through www.winespectator. com.

- Girl Scout cookies. Especially if it's now the "off-season," you'll provide a group favorite to your guests and make your daughter's, granddaughter's, niece's, or other family friends' little girl *very* happy when you order fifty boxes of Tagalongs, Samoas, or Thin Mints. (Someone's getting a badge for that!)

Living Things
- Potted herbs or kitchen garden baskets, with such herbs as thyme, rosemary, chives, and parsley for your guests' fresh cooking
- Potted flowers, like gerbera daisy plants for just a few dollars each
- Potted bamboo plants, a symbol of good luck
- A tree seedling for your guests to plant when they get home

- Flower or vegetable seed packets for gardens or borders
- Topiaries

Printed Things
- A book of love poetry or an inspirational book that's meant a lot to the two of you
- Pretty journals for your guests' gratitude lists
- Wine-tasting journals
- Travel journals
- Photo albums
- Framed quotes or bookmarks with your most valued messages on them
- A copy of your family tree, beautifully printed on parchment paper, with room left for the addition of future generations

Cultural Good Luck Charms
Use your own culture's traditions or simply borrow from another culture you admire . . .
- Korean wooden ducks, always given as a pair, to symbolize being mates for life.
- A pair of pearlized chopticks, with a note to use them on anniversaries.
- A four-leaf clover, which you can buy laminated from an Irish gift shop.
- A Celtic love knot, also available at Irish gift shops, in the form of a charm or necklace.
- A feng shui everlasting love pendant, in the form of the eternity symbol.
- Mini horseshoes or horseshoe-shaped charms, a Greek symbol of luck.
- Dolphins are a symbol of luck in New Zealand and for Australian Aborigines and Native American nations, among others.
- In China, jade is considered good luck, as is the pendant shaped in the double happiness sign, always a great choice for wedding

vow renewals. Look for small jade pendants to keep your expenses
lower.

- Elephants shown with their trunks *up* are a sign of luck in Indian
  and Asian cultures.
- Angels, of course, are positive signs, so look for angel pins and
  magnets.
- Dream catchers are a well-known Native American tradition,
  said to take away bad dreams if hung above your bed. These beautiful creations can be an extension of your wish for all of your
  guests' (good) dreams to come true.
- Religious figurines and medallions are popular favors given by
  couples who owe their relationship success to their shared faith
  and beliefs.

FOR A LITTLE ROMANCE

As the couple who has it all, and knows how to keep the romance going
strong, you might opt to give out favors that encourage all of your
guests to do the same.

- Scented massage oils in vanilla, lavender, or coconut
- Scented candles
- A book of romantic quotes or poetry
- A CD of romantic music (Chris Botti, Michael Bublé, Enigma,
  George Winston, etc.)
- Boxes of stationery, including a note from you on the importance
  of love letters
- Vases, full- or bud-sized, to encourage your guests to bring home
  flowers more often!
- Single long-stemmed roses

To each of your favors, you'll attach a printed note or label with a
note from the two of you. These do *not* take the place of an official
thank you note sent after the celebration, however. They're just a personalized touch to the take-home gift, with your thanks.

Part 5

ADDITIONAL DETAILS

DONNA AND BOB MATOSKEY, MARRIED APRIL 6, 1968,
RENEWED IN THE BAHAMAS ON APRIL 9, 2003

"We've renewed our wedding vows twice. Once for our twenty-fifth wedding anniversary, which was in the same church with the same priest who married us, and for our thirty-fifth wedding anniversary, we held it at Breezes resort in the Bahamas. We flew down with ten guests, and since we'd been going to that resort for over ten years, they really made our renewal something special for us. They arranged everything, including a minister who said he loved renewals because he knows the couple is really in love, and a professional photographer who we loved. He had a great personality, took pictures all over the place, and he got a kick out of the fact that I walked barefoot on the beach with my daughter during the processional. I call it my 'fantasy wedding,' and the pictures we have from it are so beautiful. My favorite photo is of us walking along the beach. We have a photo album, and pictures from our renewal were in the local paper, and we gave interviews for the media there. We're planning to renew our vows again for our fortieth anniversary and may go to a winery in New Jersey for that one."

18

PHOTOGRAPHY AND VIDEOGRAPHY

At the vast majority of vow renewal ceremonies and celebrations, the couple does *not* hire professional photographers and videographers. For them, it's fine to have a friend or relative take the pictures and video footage on their own digital cameras.

After all, with the advent of the digital camera and the ease of uploading, editing, creating an online photo album, and clicking a button to order prints in every size (plus mugs, magnets, mousepads, and T-shirts featuring your likeness), it's all too easy to go the do-it-yourself route. Plus, it's far, far less expensive than hiring professionals by the hour, worrying about getting the negatives in order to leave copies made, and you get your shots and footage right away.

By no means am I implying that yours is a less important party than a wedding or that hiring professional photo masters isn't for you. I'm reporting on the trend, and on the enjoyment renewal couples have in editing their own shots online and creating and e-mailing photo albums to their guests. It's a twenty-first-century trend that's hot for renewal couples. They like the power to be in their own hands in cases like these.

With complete software programs—ask a friend if he or she has a program you might be able to use *or* invest now in your own for future picture projects—you can crop your photos, reduce red-eye, turn your photos into black-and-white shots, add one color image to a black-and-white picture (such as your bright red bouquet to stand out in the black-and-white image). You can blur the edges of your borders, add graphic text in colored fonts with wavy word art or 3-D lettering, whatever you wish. These are the kinds of editing options so many brides and grooms are requesting of their professional photo experts, and you may have access to them as well.

Video footage can be edited with soundtracks and title words on the screen, and then streamed into e-mails, onto your wedding Web site, and burned onto DVDs. If you're the traditional types, you might not want your video "messed with." It may be enough for you just to have an uninterrupted, "exactly as it happened" documentary of your day in real time. You wouldn't want to lose a minute of footage through any kind of edit.

The new technologies definitely give renewal couples a break. All that's needed are reliable people to take your photos and video, plus access to great digital cameras. Here's some advice so that this personalized and budget-friendly choice goes smoothly for you.

- Ask not just one person to take the pictures, but several. It wouldn't be right to obligate a helpful friend to "work" throughout your entire event, so designate three or four people to work shifts. Two can share the digital photo camera, and two can share the video camera.

- If friends are willing to use their own top-of-the-line cameras, that's terrific. But you might choose to upgrade your own cameras now for all of your future adventures and events. If you're not camera-savvy, ask a friend or relative for advice on choosing the best models. Many couples, knowing the advantages of digital cameras in a life filled with grandkids and family vacations, consider these new cameras to be their renewal gifts to one another.

- Practice with your own camera and encourage your volunteers to do the same.

- Make sure the owners of the cameras bring extra batteries and memory chips.

- Provide your volunteers with a detailed itinerary, so that they know where pre- and post-celebration photos will be taken and can arrive on time.

- Provide your volunteers with a list of requested shots.

- Take all of the important photos right away, so that the "job" of snapping pictures or rolling camera is finished earlier in the event. When you cut your cake and do your spotlight dance earlier in the event, that completes your most-important-shot wish list. Your official photographers can set down their cameras and enjoy themselves now.

- You can also set out throwaway or one-time use cameras for your guests to use to get some great candid shots and shots of your guests.

- Use a panoramic setting on your camera. There's no better way to capture a wide-angle view of all your guests on the beach, your entire celebration, or that amazing sunset behind where you're taking your vows. Look for panoramic throwaway cameras in party supply stores, camera shops, and stores like Target and Wal-Mart.

Hiring a Professional Photographer and Videographer

You are, of course, free to skip the do-it-yourself route in favor of hiring a professional photographer and videographer for your vow renewal event. Especially if you're among those planning the formal "wedding you never had" with the very best of everything that most first-time brides and grooms only dream about planning.

It's a fabulous, high-tech world out there right now for professional photographers and videographers. Most have gone digital, and camera technologies have vastly improved in the past five years. So if you married before then, you might find yourselves with many new technology and editing options. Today's experts can do things they never could before, such as posting your proofs online for your review and ordering, and sharing that collection with your guests so that they can order the shots they want to—all just a few days after the wedding. No more waiting three to six months for film to go to a lab before you get your first look.

Where to Find the Best Photographers and Videographers

- Check with recently married friends and family members for their recommendations.
- Check with your wedding coordinator and other wedding vendors for referrals.
- Collect names from the professional organizations the pros belong to: Professional Photographers of America, www.ppa.com, 800–786–6277; Wedding and Portrait Photographers International, www.eventphotographers.com; Professional Videographer Association of America, www.pva.to, 209–653–8307; Wedding and Event Videographers Association International, www.weva .com; International Special Event Society (photographers and videographers are members), www.ises.com.

Interviewing Potential Photo and Video Experts

- When you've collected your potential candidates, you'll first need to find out which kind of style or school of photography and videography they represent. There's a vast difference in the industry, due to the professionals' most natural feel for their work. Some are designated as *portrait-style*, where they focus on posed portraits and gathering shots. Other are *candid-style*, where they'd prefer to skip the posed shots and just capture all those magical moments as they happen. And others are *photojournalistic-style*, where their choices of shots and footage capture the story of your day. You'll find more photos and footage of things like the scenery around the trellis where you'll take your vows, your bouquet sitting on a table, silhouette shots of you walking into the distance. Look at their sample albums and videos and talk to them about which style they subscribe to. Then see if their style matches yours.

WORDS FROM A PROFESSIONAL

I spoke with Scott Rodgers, principal photographer from Stuart-Rodgers Photography in Chicago (www.srphoto.com) about what he's capturing at wedding vow renewals today.

We're taking a lot of location shots with couples and their kids. Not those posed family photos where everyone is standing in a line and smiling. It's more interactive, where I capture the family members talking or laughing, the kids playing together, those spontaneous shots that show a family's dimensions and personality. We might go to the beach for a session, for instance, and in no time at all I've taken three hundred pictures of the family interacting. The albums we create reflect that, and it shows more of who you are than a traditional posed picture could ever do.

- Look through their samples thoroughly. See if certain images jump out at you and if video montages are seamless and footage conveys something original.
- Ask about their price and per-hour packages. Some experts charge in the higher stratosphere, and some offer budget packages with a small timeframe, such as three-hour package rather than a five-hour.
- Ask about their technology and equipment. See if they're using the latest models and have them explain what they can do for you with them.
- Ask about development. Do they develop on-site or send to a lab? How long will video-editing procedures take?
- Ask if they'll bring assistants to your event. Many experts do bring along an apprentice or assistant to help them juggle all of their cameras, batteries, film bags, tripods, and the like. If an assistant will be there, you'll have to add that person to your guest list. And remember that your photographer, videographer, and any assistants must be added to your guest list headcount for the caterer.
- Provide them with an itinerary so that they arrive in time to take their shots.

- Ask them what their travel and overtime fees are, as well as their refund and cancellation policies.
- Ask what they will be wearing, and share the formality level and style of your event. You wouldn't want your photographer to be in a suit while everyone else is dressed informally, for instance.
- See if they work outside. Some might have a policy of not shooting outdoor or beach events, as a way to protect their equipment.
- Ask about purchasing your negatives. Some experts will allow you to buy your negatives, so that you can buy duplicates or make enlargements on your own.
- Ask about liability insurance. Every good expert should have a policy.

A SUGGESTION FROM PROFESSIONAL PHOTOGRAPHER
SCOTT RODGERS

> *One of the things vow renewal couples like to do is to re-pose a photo from their original wedding. Perhaps they had a picture in a family garden, where it was the bride and groom and their parents, their brothers and sisters. Now, years later, we'll gather all the same people together at the exact same spot, in the same order, and add in the meaningful addition of new family members like kids, babies, new spouses.*

JENNIFER AND GREG GRIZZLE, MARRIED OCTOBER 19, 1991,

RENEWED OCTOBER 19, 1996

"We wanted to reward all of our guests who traveled out to Las Vegas for our intentionally 'very Vegas' wedding vow renewal, so we booked two stretch limousines to use on our big night out. On the way to the ceremony, we planned the white one for the ladies and a black one for the men. After the ceremony, we all piled into whichever limousine we liked and we headed out for a night on the town, including dinner and dancing until 4:00 a.m. at the Club Rio at the Rio Hotel."

19

TRANSPORTATION

A sleek, black limousine. A shining white Bentley. A horse and carriage. If you did it before, you can do it again. There's no rule that says you can't book the same kinds of luxury or classic car, or fairy-tale romance rides that you first took to the chapel for your wedding vow renewal ceremony. Or, if you didn't get the chance back then to book a limo, now's your time!

Granted, many couples do skip this category . . . and its expense. If the renewal event will be held in its entirety at home or at a hotel or restaurant, there's no need to arrange transportation at all. No wheels needed. Besides the time saved, you're also looking at several hundred dollars back in your pocket.

But if you're among the couples who look forward to the ride in a classic car or a stretch Lincoln Navigator or stretch Humvee, know that the world of luxury car rentals has recently opened up to include some very attractive options. While it may seem like husbands are the ones salivating over the chance to take a spin in a Ferrari, it's just as often the wives who run onto the exotic car rental lot with breathless anticipation. "I always wanted to ride in one of these!" says one who wrote to me about her dream spin in a Lotus Esprit. "It's the car from *Pretty Woman!*" Granted, this is one area that both husbands and wives really enjoy working on, and it's also the one most often chosen for a Big Surprise. That's right . . . both wives and husbands are surprising each other with rentals of exotic or classic cars as an unexpected gift on the big day. "We stepped outside to go to the church, and there was a cherry-red Corvette convertible sitting in the driveway. I handed him the key, and he just hugged me and hugged me. He said he always wanted to drive one of those, just once, since he was a little boy."

Just look at the list of "rides" available for rental these days:

Luxury and Exotic Cars

Porsche 911	Porsche Boxter	BMW 24	BMW X5
Jaguar XK-8	Jaguar S Type	Ferrari F355 Spyder	Ferrari Modena
Hummer H-2	Lexus GS 300 or 400	Dodge Viper	Corvette 206
Audi TT Convertible	Mercedes SL500	Mustang GT Convertible	Mini Cooper

Traditional Bridal Cars

Limousine	Rolls-Royce	Bentley

Unique Forms of Transportation

You read about a few unique transportation options in the chapter on closing moments, and a yacht or motorcycle could be the best way out for you. Here are some of the most-often requested modes of transport:

Horse and carriage rides

Horse and sleigh

Hot air balloon

Trolley rides

Party buses (like a nightclub on wheels, complete with leather seats, plasma screen TV, mood lighting, even a wet bar and great sound system)

A yacht

The Business of Transportation Rentals

If you've never rented a limo, classic car, or horse and carriage, you'll need to know the tips on smart booking.

- Always ask friends and family for referrals. Whom did they use

not just for weddings, but for airport pickups or corporate events?
A hotel's concierge can also recommend the reputable company
they use for their VIP guests.

- Call around to locate the kind of car or carriage you have in mind,
  but always go in person to check out the merchandise. Inspect the
  cars or carriage and know that you can request *a specific one* that
  you like for its design or interior features.
- Always request that the vehicle be washed and waxed before your
  event.
- Read the fine print on your purchase order or contract. Know the
  exact hours or time limit of your use, when overtime starts, and
  how much overtime will cost you. Insider secret: the clock starts
  when the car leaves their lot, not when it gets to your house.
- Ask what the driver will be wearing, and request a certain formality level if you wish.
- Make sure the drivers will have two-way radios as well as cell
  phones on them.
- Ask about specialty price packages aside from their three-hour
  deals.
- Provide a detailed itinerary of who gets picked up and dropped off
  where and when.
- Call to confirm the week before your event, just to be sure you're
  still all set.

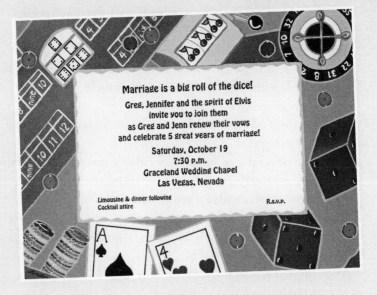

Marriage is a big roll of the dice!

Greg, Jennifer and the spirit of Elvis
invite you to join them
as Greg and Jenn renew their vows
and celebrate 5 great years of marriage!

Saturday, October 19
7:30 p.m.
Graceland Wedding Chapel
Las Vegas, Nevada

Limousine & dinner following
Cocktail attire

R.s.v.p.

JENNIFER AND GREG GRIZZLE, MARRIED OCTOBER 19, 1991,

RENEWED OCTOBER 19, 1996

"We wanted to pull out all the stops and have a kitschy, cheesy Vegas invitation for our destination vow renewal trip to Las Vegas, and we found this design with dice and cards around the border. We loved the saying 'marriage is a roll of the dice,' and we loved it for its ultra-touristy theme. It fit our celebration perfectly, and we carried that theme through our entire celebration."

20

INVITATIONS

Very few party-prep moments are as exciting as creating the invitations for your renewal celebration (well, except for maybe going for cake tastings). We'll talk about designing your beautiful and personalized invitations in a moment, but first let's tackle the big question: how to word your invitations.

Getting the Words Right

What's fabulous for you is that you'll avoid all of those incredibly detailed wedding world rules about how to word invitations. Since you're already married, there are no longer any burning questions or family diplomacy issues about how to list your parents in which order, and so on. You're the guests of honor and the hosts, so the basic model for a renewal ceremony and celebration invitation reads as follows:

> *The pleasure of your company*
> *is requested at the reaffirmation of the*
> *wedding vows of*
> *Mr. & Mrs. Jeffrey Brown*
> *on Saturday the fifth of September*
> *at seven o'clock*
> *at the Skywood Botanical Gardens*
> *Los Angeles, California*
> *Reception immediately following ceremony*
> *R.S.V.P.*

The R.S.V.P. at the bottom of this invitation may be surprising to you, as in, "Hey, I thought that was taken care of in a response card!" You're absolutely correct to notice the change. Now, you can either do a response card in the same model as a wedding invitation or add the R.S.V.P. to your invitation. Both options work, and you may add your phone number to the model above.

You'll use the "Mr. and Mrs. Jeffrey Brown" title for you as a couple as a matter of formality. This is the proper form of identifying yourselves as a couple, according to traditional etiquette. Of course, if you wish to bend etiquette a little bit, you may certainly list yourselves on *less formal* invitations as Jeffrey and Carol Brown.

If your name is hyphenated, you'd write Mr. Jeffrey Brown and Mrs. Carol Jenkins-Brown. It might be important to you to honor the name you go by, perhaps your professional name. If this is your choice, it's your own rule to make.

When Your Children Are the Hosts

In some instances, the children of the couple are throwing the celebration. It was their idea, and they've planned the whole thing from the location to the menu to the décor to the entertainment. They've also paid for it. It's their baby. So they'll be listed on the invitation as follows:

> *Sarah Allen, Maria Allen, and Mark Allen*
> *request the pleasure of your company*
> *as their parents*
> *Reginald and Marsha Allen*
> *renew their wedding vows*
> *[then follow the traditional model with date, time, and location]*

If the children are married and hosting the celebration as couples, they would be listed together with their spouses. When it's a husband-wife team, many wives choose to include their maiden names on the invitation, even if they do not regularly hyphenate them. This step is a

service to guests (such as friends, bosses and clients of their parents)
who will then be able to more easily identify them:

> *George Winters and Sarah Allen-Winters*
> *Kenneth and Maria Allen Dubrowski*
> *and Mark and Tina Allen*
> *request the pleasure of your company*
> *[etc.]*

Post-Renewal Celebrations

If you've decided to run off to Tahiti to renew your vows in private, or
with just your kids along for the vacation (and perhaps a surprise renewal!), you may wish to celebrate with all of your friends and family
after-the-fact. You certainly can throw a big party later! Even brides
and grooms who take a half dozen guests away for their destination
weddings are doing the same thing: marry now, have the big party
later. If this is your plan, here's your invitation *and announcement*
model:

> *The pleasure of your company*
> *is requested at a reaffirmation party*
> *celebrating a recent renewal of*
> *wedding vows of*
> *Mr. & Mrs. Andrew French*
> *on Saturday the ninth of April*
> *at seven o'clock*
> *at the Knoll Alumni Club*
> *Cincinnati, Ohio*
> *Reception immediately following ceremony*
> *R.S.V.P.*

If You're Inviting Guests to a Destination Ceremony

Your invitation will read the same as the regular model, with the addition of more location details. For instance, you might include:

at the Southampton Princess
on the island of Bermuda

If you'll send out less formal invitations, which might be your choice of style, you can word your message with excitement:

Come fly away with us to Bermuda!
We're renewing our wedding vows
on the pink sand beaches
and we'd love to have you join us!
Flying date: Saturday, March third
Ceremony and party date: Sunday morning, March fourth
Flyback date: Monday morning, March fifth
R.S.V.P. for hotel block information

Some Rules About Invitations

While you get to avoid many of the traditional bridal etiquette hassles, you'll still need to abide by general rules of special event etiquette.

- You may send invitations to couples and their kids.
- If "the kids" are over the age of eighteen, they each get their own invitations.
- *All* single guests over the age of eighteen should be allowed to bring a date, so tack on an "and Guest" for each. It's just bad form not to, and some singles take it as a high insult when you don't.
- You'll address your guests by their official titles for formal invitations, such as Dr. Kristen Lamonte or Commander David Lintell.
- When you're inviting couples with their kids, you'll address the invitation to them as follows: *Mr. and Mrs. Nicholas Grant and Family* or *Mr. and Mrs. Nicholas Grant, Anne, Thomas, and Daniel.*
- Make sure you know the names and correct spellings for all guests and their kids. Check with other relatives if you're not sure that a cousin has three rather than two kids. This extra step for protocol

prevents any embarrassment on your part or hurt feelings on a guest's part.

- When you're inviting adults only, as in the case of a formal celebration where kids wouldn't be comfortable, you'll convey this message by the wording on the envelope: *Mr. and Mrs. Nicholas Grant.* They'll know from that wording to get a babysitter for the day of your event.

- You'll also want to make sure you know the correct marital status for guests. Talk with friends or relatives to make sure you have everyone's status correct.

- For formal invitations, you'll spell out all abbreviations (such as *Street,* rather than *St.,* *Avenue* rather than *Ave.*) and numbers (*fifth,* rather than 5th).

- For informal invitations, you may use abbreviations if you wish.

- The rule for *honor* vs. *honour?* If your ceremony will be held in a house of worship, that's when the formal-looking British spelling *honour* (or *favour*) is used. This rule applies more to weddings, but you may certainly claim it as your own as well, particularly if you're having a do-over renewal event.

Additional Invitation Inserts

If you'll create formal invitation packets, you might choose to follow the model that brides and grooms are using and enclose separate inserts with your invitations. Here are your guidelines.

Reception Card—Reception cards provide all of the details for the celebration.

Response Card—To be used by your guests as an official R.S.V.P. to you. They'll fill in their names on the line and then check whether they will or won't attend, plus their choice of meal if one is offered.

Maps or Directions—Provide a printout of driving directions to your ceremony and reception sites. Most banquet halls and ballrooms, plus houses of worship, will provide you with small squares of paper with driving directions if you ask; otherwise, it's up to you to create them.

Additional Items to Print

As a matter of style, you may also choose to create the following:

Menu Cards—Placed on each guest table, the menu card will present the upcoming courses by name and perhaps by ingredient (such as letting guests know those are indeed lobster ravioli).

Place Cards—Using specialty place card pages found at the office supply store, you'll follow an easy template to print out your own tear-apart cards featuring each guest's name and table number. Personalize or accent the cards as you wish.

Favor Cards—Featuring your names and the date of your event or a thank you message.

Ceremony Programs—Each program lists the names of everyone involved (from the officiant to your bridal party attendants to musical performers) and an explanation of each segment of your ceremony. You might list the titles and composers of special songs that will be performed, along with a brief description of the song's significance to you. Do you need to have a program? No, it's not a must. But it is a feature that many renewal couples are using to convey all of the deeper meanings and sentimental stories that their ceremonies include.

Save the Date Cards—If your event will take place during a busy summer season, or around the time of a major holiday, it's a wise idea to send out "save the date" cards. This simple card or postcard will announce to your invited guests that they should reserve the weekend of your renewal celebration ahead of time. You can provide hotel room block information and links, as well as a link to your personalized or family Web site, if you wish, on the back of the card for your guests' use.

Now, Let's Design Your Invitations!

Now that you know the elements of your invitation packet, and the additional items you'll print up for your day, it's time to choose your style. After all, you may wish to coordinate your individual items in the same design, perhaps ordering them professionally as a full set. Whether it's you working creatively at your computer, trying out fonts and colors, or a professional invitation artist working magic with your requests, the questions are the same. Here you'll design your invitations from start to finish.

Invitation Card Shape—Square cards are the hottest trend right now, even for formal wedding do-over invitations. You can choose any shape and size you like, from circular to oval to pyramid-shaped, and traditional rectangular. Be aware that square and larger invitations, plus thicker card stocks, usually require extra postage.

Card Thickness—Most cards are of the thinner card stock variety (all the cheaper to ship them in packets), but you'll also find thicker card stocks available.

Number of Panels—Choose from a single card (called a "panel") with the words printed only on the front, a dual-fold greeting card style, a trifold, or a more creative origami style, such as an invitation that folds out into the shape of a heart or a butterfly.

Type of Print—Know the difference between the appearance of different types of printed processes. Engraved is the most formal of the bunch, with raised lettering that leaves reverse indentations on the back of the card. Thermography is the one you see on the average wedding invitation, while offset or flatbed printing provides a lovely type in unraised lettering at a lower price point. Calligraphy gives a personalized touch to your invitations as well and can be created on your home computer as well as by hand.

Type of Font—Ask to see printouts of the invitation designer's available fonts, which are the shape and design of the letters and numbers themselves. (Be sure to see what the fonts look like in all letters and numbers to be sure the artistic design renders you able to tell a *T* from a *J*, for instance.)

Color of Print—Colored ink is all the rage right now, even for the most formal weddings, which used to call for strictly black lettering on ecru paper. Etiquette rules have bent to allow for colored ink on colored paper stock.

YOUR ART PAPER SOURCE
> One great source to check is www.artpaper.com for such amazing finds as handmade papers from Japan, Thailand, Nepal, and other worldly locations.

Vellums—These simple semitranslucent overlay sheets provide an extra dash of color, and a special accent to even the simplest and most elegant printed packet. At www.artpaper.com, for instance, you'll find ink-jet and laser printer friendly vellums in such solid colors as cream, light blue, celadon, seafoam green, pastel pink, and orange.

Ribbon Accents—Punch a pair of holes close together at the top of your invitation panel and tie a tiny bow with a short length of color-coordinated ribbon. Also popular: using a creatively shaped hole punch to make the openings for the ribbon bow or just as a unique accent.

Borders—You'll find a range of blush colors, with graphics such as hearts, daisies, vines, ivy (symbolizing fidelity and wedded bliss), dots, and even chic stripes and paisley.

Graphics—Your invitations and programs can include terrific color or black-and-white graphics that you'll upload from your own digital camera or picture files you already have. They can be great shots of you both, a picture from your wedding, a full family photo together with your kids, or just a great scenery shot like that amazing rainbow you captured arcing over the ocean. Use your own photo editing software (it may have come with your digital camera software), to add effects to your picture. You might blur the edges or turn it into a sepia tone, or use digital hand-painting to add just a few bursts of color to a black-and-white photo.

Order or Make-It-Yourself?

If you'll order professionally made invitations, place your order at least five months before your event to allow plenty of time for creation and shipping. Check out reputable invitations companies by asking re-cently married friends or family for their referrals, and check out my favorites: www.invitations4sale.com and (for custom work) www. VismaraInvitations.com. Another top choice that I love is www. PSAEssentials.com, where you'll find very trendy, adorable invitation styles and terrific prices. Work with your invitation stylist to personal-ize your choices, see a print proof (print is always a better choice than an e-mailed proof, as you'll get a better look at the final product), and of course make sure all of your information is correct before you order.

If you'll make your own invitations, be sure to allow plenty of pro-duction time. This process is to be enjoyed, so allow time for relaxed designing and printing evenings, packet assembly, and envelope stuff-ing. Most renewal couples tackle this job as a team, perhaps with a great glass of wine or mug of coffee in hand, making it an event in it-self. Kids can help, as can friends, if you have a large guest list or lots of crafty personalizing to do.

YOUR DO-IT-YOURSELF-INVITATION SOFTWARE SOURCE
Check out www.mountaincow.com for easy invitation-making software, including modern fonts, graphics, and monogram accents.

It's a Postage Thing

Just as you did with your wedding invitations, you'll take one of your bigger or bulkier invitation packets to the post office for a test weighing to find out the amount of postage required for each. You might have gone over the weight limit *or* a large or odd size of en-velope might require extra postage. It's best to be safe and get the weigh-in.

Once you're sure of your postage situation, you can then pick out pretty themed stamps for your envelopes. Check out the postal service's Web site, www.usps.gov, to select from their specialty stamps, which you can choose to match your party's theme. You might go with the current crop of Love stamps, or ones with flowers on them, or architectural stamps, ones featuring classic cars, trains, boats—your choice. There are more options listed on the site than are displayed in most post offices, and you can order your stamps online rather than stand in line. You can also get personalized postage stamps bearing your choice of digital photo at www.photostamps.com.

Another popular option for vow renewal couples is selecting a stamp that gives back. You'll find the breast cancer stamp with the pink ribbon for a slightly higher price than the going rate for first-class stamps, for instance. The difference is donated to the cause. If you're charitable-minded, this could be an opportunity to give a little back.

SPEAKING OF CHARITABLE CAUSES

Why not set up a charitable gift registry? It's not considered proper to register for gifts for a renewel ceremony, even though you know your guests will want to get you something you can use. What you *can* do, as a matter of gracious hosting, is set up a charitable registry and list it on your family's Web site (or on a personalized Web site for your renewal, such as www.WedStudio.com). You'll add a note about your support of a certain charity or cause and request that guests consider donating in lieu of presenting you with any gifts.

Check out the charitable gift registry programs at www.IDoFoundation.org and www.JustGive.org, two of the leading charitable registries out there. Or, share a link to a relative or friend's charity-run Web site. Wouldn't it be wonderful if your renewal guests all found a link to your niece's Team in Training Web site, to raise money to battle blood cancers like lymphoma and leukemia? You know that she needs to raise $4,000 in order to participate in her first marathon in Alaska, so you're directing support to her admirable and inspiring efforts as a way for *your* marriage to help *her* help the *cause*. Providing her Team in Training site is all you need to do, with a note stating how proud you are of her and how much that charity means to you. Guests will understand, and again, it's their choice if they want to participate. They could always get you that bottle of wine or bouquet of flowers.

EPILOGUE: CARRYING ON THE TRADITION

SUSANNE ALEXANDER AND CRAIG FARNSWORTH, MARRIED AUGUST 28, 1999,
RENEWED AUGUST 28, 2004

After your vow renewel ceremony, you can make your new vows, or the practice of re-stating your commitments, an annual gift to one another. You'll carry on the ritual of renewing your vows, perhaps even making it an adventure to do so in all the places you travel in the future. Here is the story of a couple who did just that.

"We celebrated our fifth anniversary this year in a special and meaningful way. We left the Midwest and traveled to Lover's Point Park in Pacific

Grove, California, a romantic and intimate spot overlooking the ocean and rocky coastline. Sitting on a bench under the sun, we watched couples and families enjoy life and even saw a wedding rehearsal in progress. This was very fitting, as we sat there together renewing our own wedding vows.

"Before we married, we explored and wrote down seventeen statements of what we were committed to in a marriage together. These included treating one another and our children with love, respect, and courtesy; being of service to others; being playful, having fun, and incorporating humor into our daily life; and maintaining our relationship through difficulties. We included these commitments in our wedding program and read them to our guests. Each year for our anniversary, we assess how well we are doing or if we need to take new actions. Together, we pray, repeat our wedding vows, and then alternate reading these commitments, reaffirming once again we love being married to one another."

Susanne Alexander and Craig Farnsworth's marriage commitments expanded into creating the Marriage Transformation Project to support others in maintaining happy, lasting marriages (www.marriage transformation.com).

NOTE FROM THE AUTHOR

Congratulations! Few things in life are more admirable than a couple who can make a marriage work, bring the best of themselves to their partnership, agree to disagree, and weather the storms of life to emerge true to their wedding vows.

As I mentioned at the start of this book, it's my honor to have helped you plan a celebration of your marriage. I lift a champagne toast to the two of you and wish you an amazing future together, continued excitement and adventure on the road ahead, and a life filled with blessings. You've been a tremendous example to your family and friends, showing them what real love and commitment look like, and they'll learn from you. They say the best legacy possible to leave your family is the love you expressed . . . to them, and to each other.

When you reseal your wedding vows with a kiss, no matter what your ceremony or reception may be like, you're experiencing a moment that's golden to both of you. It's all in that one moment. Every promise, every challenge overcome, every wonderful memory and the reaffirmation that you belong together. All we have with our loved ones are moments—collections of them. This is your moment. Enjoy it to the fullest!

With all best wishes for continued joy,
Sharon Naylor

RESORCES

This list is purely for your research use, and does not imply endorsement or recommendation of the companies or products. Since Web sites change over the course of time, we apologize if any Web addresses have changed since the time of this printing.

Wedding Planning Web Sites

Bliss Weddings: www.blissweddings.com

Bridal Guide: www.bridalguide.com

Martha Stewart Weddings:

www.marthastewart.com

Town and Country Weddings (upscale):

www.townandcountry.com

Wedding Channel:

www.weddingchannel.com

Gowns

After Six: www.aftersix.com

Alfred Angelo: www.alfredangelo.com

Bill Levkoff: www.billlevkoff.com

Bloomingdales: www.bloomingdales.com

Champagne Formals:

www.champagneformals.com

David's Bridal: www.davidsbridal.com

Dessy Creations: www.dessy.com

Henry Roth: www.henryroth.com

JC Penney: www.jcpenney.com

Jessica McClintock:

www.jessicamcclintock.com

Jim Hjelm Designs:

www.jimhjelmoccasions.com

Macy's: www.macys.com

Michelle Roth: www.micheleroth.com

Melissa Sweet Bridal:

www.melissasweet.com

Mori Lee: www.morileeinc.com

Spiegel: www.spiegel.com

Vera Wang: www.verawang.com

Watters and Watters: www.watters.com

Shoes and Accessories

David's Bridal: www.davidsbridal.com

Dyeables: www.dyeables.com

Fenaroli for Regalia: www.fenaroli.com

JC Penney: www.jcpenney.com

Kenneth Cole: www.kennethcole.com

Nina Footwear: www.ninashoes.com

Salon Shoes: www.salonshoes.com

Watters and Watters: www.watters.com

Jewelry

A Diamond is Forever:

www.adiamondisforever.com

American Gem Society: www.ags.org

Blue Nile: www.bluenile.com

Cartier: www.cartier.com

Diamond.com: www.diamond.com

Diamond Cutters International:

www.diamondcuttersintl.com

Ice.com: www.ice.com

Jewelry Information Center: www.jic.org

Jewelry.com: www.jewelry.com

Paul Klecka: www.klecka.com

Tiffany: www.tiffany.com

Zales: www.zales.com

Invitations

An Invitation to Buy Nationwide:

www.invitations4sale.com

Anna Griffin Invitation Design:

www.annagriffin.com

Botanical Paper Works:

www.botanicalpaperworks.com

Crane and Company: www.crane.com

Evangel Christian Invitations:

www.evangelwedding.com

Invite Site (made from recycled paper):

www.invitesite.com

MountainCow: www.mountaincow.com

Now and Forever: www.now-and-

forever.com

PaperStyle.com: www.paperstyle.com

Papyrus: www.papyrusonline.com

Precious Collection:

www.preciouscollection.com

PSA Essentials: www.psaessentials.com

Vismara Invitations:

www.vismarainvitations.com

You're Invited: www.youreinvited.com

Linens

Chair Covers Online:

www.chaircoversonline.com

Source One: www.sourceone.com

Live Butterflies

Butterfly Celebration:

www.butterflycelebration.com

Swallowtail Farms:

www.swallowtailfarms.com

Music and Entertainment

Piano Brothers: www.pianobrothers.com

Wedding Channel:

www.weddingchannel.com

Amazon: www.amazon.com

Barnes and Noble: www.bn.com

Lyrics Depot: www.lyricsdepot.com

Lyrics Freak: www.lyricsfreak.com

Romantic Lyrics: www.romantic-lyrics.com

Sing 365: www.sing365.com

Music in the Air (New York City area):

www.musicintheair.com

Flowers and Greenery

HGTV: www.hgtv.com

P. Allen Smith: www.pallensmith.com

About.com: www.about.com

Romantic Flowers:

www.romanticflowers.com

Botanicals: www.botanicalschicago.com

Favors

Godiva: www.godiva.com

Charming Favours:
www.charmingfavours.com

Beau-Coup: www.beau-coup.com

Bella Terra: www.bellaterra.net

Cheryl&Co (cookies, brownies, amazing
sweets): www.cherylandco.com

Illuminations: www.illuminations.com

Kebobs.com: www.kebobs.com

Lender Ink: www.lenderink.com

M&M's: www.mms.com

Moma Store: www.momastore.org

My Wedding Labels:
www.myweddinglabels.com

PajamaGram: www.pajamagram.com

Pearl River (Asian): www.pearlriver.com

Pepper People: www.pepperpeople.com

Pier 1: www.pier1.com

Surfa's (gourmet food):
www.surfasonline.com

Wedding Things: www.weddingthings.com

Zingerman's (gourmet food):
www.zingermans.com

Gourmet and Food

Cheryl&Co: www.cherylandco.com

Fizzy Lizzy: www.fizzylizzy.com

Gail Watson: www.gailwatsoncakes.com

Izze: www.izze.com

Personal Chef Association:
www.personalchef.com

Ron Ben-Israel Wedding Cakes:
www.weddingcakes.com

Surfas: www.surfasonline.com

Steazsoda: www.steazsoda.com

Wilton's (cake and cupcake supplies):
www.wiltons.com

Zingerman's: www.zingermans.com

The Food Network: www.foodtv.com

Caterers and Chefs

International Association of Culinary
Professionals: www.iacp.com

International Special Events Society:
www.ises.com

National Association of Catering Executives:
www.nace.net

Personal Chef Association:
www.personalchef.com

Rentals

American Rental Association:
www.ararental.org

Warehouse Stores

BJ's Wholesale Club: www.bjs.com

Costco: www.costco.com

Sam's Club: www.samsclub.com

Crafts and Paper

Michaels: www.michaels.com

Scrapjazz: www.scapjazz.com

Flax Art: www.flaxart.com

Office Max: www.officemax.com

Staples: www.staples.com

My Wedding Labels:
www.myweddinglabels.com

Paper Access: www.paperaccess.com

Paper Direct: www.paperdirect.com

Online Invitations

Evite: www.evite.com

Hallmark: www.hallmark.com

Blue Mountain Arts:

    www.bluemountain.com

Travel

Tourism Office Worldwide Directory:

    www.towd.com

ATMS Travel News (adventure getaways):

    www.atmstravelnews.com

Amtrak: www.amtrak.com

Expedia: www.expedia.com

Travelocity: www.travelocity.com

Travel Zoo: www.travelzoo.com

VRBO (vacation house or condo rentals):

    www.vrbo.com

Sandals: www.sandals.com

Couples: www.couples.com

Hilton: www.hilton.com

IberoStar: www.iberostar.com

Occidental: www.occidentalhotels.com

Palace Resorts: www.palaceresorts.com

SuperClubs: www.superclubs.com

Charmed Places: www.charmedplaces.com

Porthole Magazine: www.porthole.com

Travel and Leisure Magazine (World's Best

    awards): www.travelandleisure.com

Bed and Breakfasts

www.bbonline.com

www.bnbfinder.com

www.bnblist.com

www.theinnkeeper.com

www.vacationspot.com

Wine and Champagne

www.winespectator.com

Special Event Association

(find your event-planning experts here)

Association of Bridal Consultants:

    www.bridalassn.com

International Special Event Society:

    www.ises.com

Professional Photographers of America:

    www.ppa.com, 800-786-6277

Wedding and Portrait Photographers

    International:

    www.eventphotographers.com

Professional Videographer Association of

    America: www.pva.to, 209-653-8307

Wedding & Event Videographers Association

    International: www.weva.com

Wedding Officiants:

    www.weddingofficiants.com

Weather and Sunset

Sunset Time (find the precise sunset time for

    any day of the year): www.usno.navy.mil

Weather Channel:

    www.weatherchannel.com

INDEX

© RICH PENROSE

SHARON NAYLOR has written twenty-eight wedding-planning books and two bridal-themed novels. She has appeared as a wedding expert on *Nightline*, *Lifetime*, *Inside Edition*, *ABC News*, *Fox 5 News*, and on hundreds of radio stations nationally and internationally, as well as in *Wedding Channel Magazine*, *Bridal Guide*, *Bride's*, *Southern Bride*, *Redbook*, and many other national magazines. She is also a columnist at *Vow* magazine and SheKnows.com, a contributing editor at *Bridal Guide*, the first wedding author featured on BlissWeddings.com's guest expert forum, and the longtime Q&A expert at NJWedding.com as well as a wedding-content contributor for Bed Bath & Beyond. Her Web site is www.sharonnaylor.net and she is the founder of the first national Book Club for Brides, featuring wedding-themed novels. She lives in Madison, New Jersey, and is at work on her upcoming wedding and family celebration titles.